# The Hymns
## of
# W. Vernon Higham

# The
# Hymns
# of
# W. Vernon Higham

Tentmaker Publications
Stoke-on-Trent
1998

# Tentmaker Publications
121 Harsthill Road, Stoke-on-Trent, Staffordshire, ST4 7LU.

ISBN 1 899003 24 4

Previous collections of the hymns of W. Vernon Higham
have included:

*Giving Thanks: A collection of English and Welsh Hymns*
(1968, The Evangelical Movement of Wales)

*Joy Unspeakable: A further collection of English and Welsh Hymns*
(The Evangelical Movement of Wales)

*Making Melody*
(1981, The Heath Christian Trust)

This collection contains all the English hymns from the previous
books plus an additional twenty-two hymns.

Binding by
Sovereign Bookcare
Stoke-on-Trent

# A Personal Testimony

At a time when the Christian faith is at a low ebb and the thought of godliness is not acceptable, it may seem strange to be producing some simple hymns that express a longing for God and for His influence upon our lives. Nevertheless, it has been my desire from my early days in the Christian faith to write at least one hymn of some spiritual value. All my life I have loved the rich Welsh hymnology of my background. It is my earnest prayer that some of these hymns will speak to others and encourage fellow believers on their spiritual pilgrimage.

I was born in Caernarfon, in North Wales, my mother being a native of that town, whereas my father hailed from the North of England. The language of the town and of my friends was Welsh. My home was bilingual, although my brother and I spoke Welsh to each other. During the depression of the 1930s life was hard for everyone. In one sense as a family we were comfortably established as compared with most. Our family owned and ran a grocery and also a small farm two miles out of the town. Nevertheless we lived in a time of great poverty and no business could really succeed. Added to this was my father's failing health. Eventually the family moved to Lancashire, my father's home county, and for the next stage of my life Bolton was to be my home. It was a great wrench to move from a market town to a large industrial town, from a place where everyone knew one another to a place which seemed so big and so full of strangers. There was the task of settling into a new school and also the change of language to cope with. Perhaps loneliness was the main problem I encountered and, because of this, my brother and I became companions as well as brothers, despite the five year gap between our ages.

Spiritually I had known nothing other than every family who attended the means of grace. The majority of any congregation in my home town in Wales were people who experienced the great Revival of 1904. I really believed that all grown-up people were godly folk. The Sabbath day was special and I must say that I truly loved the house of God, although I was often in trouble because of my mischievous nature. Whilst in Caernarfon I went with my grandmother to her chapel on Sunday evenings, having been with my parents to another in the morning and afternoon. I remember very little of what was said but I had my favourite preachers. Two qualities I particularly admired at that time were illustrations and brevity! In all this, however, the influence of my grandmother was very strong in my life. Despite the fact that I was but 7 when she died, her words remained. She would often take me with her as she visited her friends. Her conversation was always about the Lord and the marvellous works and transformation of lives she had seen during the Revival. I found it both thrilling and fascinating and to this day I have such a clear impression of her that the memory of her words seems but a few years ago. In addition I cannot omit mentioning my parents and their devotion to the things of God who, in His mercy, in later life visited them with saving grace.

After moving house several times, which for me also meant changing schools, we eventually found our spiritual home in the Welsh Calvinistic Methodist chapel in Bolton, which was part of the Welsh Presbytery of Manchester. Although there were many other Welsh denominations in the area which offered love and friendship generally, we remained in our own, and the chapel in Bolton soon became the very centre of my life. We had left Caernarfon in 1939 when I was 12 and before long a great war broke out that was to change all our lives. Times of fear occurred during air-raids, times of sorrow came with untimely deaths. We experienced times of great fellow-feeling, and long dark winters when all stayed at home in the evenings. I believe that in those days family life became particularly important. It was our custom to walk together to chapel on Sunday morning as there was no bus service. We walked there again for Sunday School, followed by an early evening service.

There was also a weekly prayer-meeting followed by a meeting called 'Y Seiat' (The Fellowship Meeting) and one of my clearest memories regarding spiritual things was being asked by the Elders to write an essay on the 1859 Revival and read it to the members. I was 14 at the time! I can recall searching through the bound copies of Welsh magazines of the nineteenth century and reading the weekly accounts of that Revival. My heart was won, and though I remember nothing of the meeting apart from the dread I felt as I sat in the front row waiting to be called to speak, from that time onwards Revival became my greatest desire.

Towards the end of the war I served in the coal mines, as most conscripts did at that late stage. Then afterwards I applied to train as a school teacher in the college at Carmarthen in South Wales. I thoroughly enjoyed my time there. I loved the place and the company of men from all parts of South Wales. I applied myself to my work and enjoyed the times in schools during teaching practice. Following this I taught Welsh in a school in Cardiff, where I made many friends. One, in particular, was a young man like myself from North Wales. We were both faithful to our respective chapels and, whenever we met, we would talk about the things of God. The outcome of this was that we both resolved to serve God in some capacity. They were precious days for me.

I returned home to teach at a school a few miles from Bolton, and I must say that I thoroughly enjoyed my work, especially teaching Art. I well remember standing on my own in the classroom one day and recalling to mind my promise to serve God. By that time I was the superintendent of the Sunday School in the Welsh Chapel and had even been appointed an elder in my early twenties! Nevertheless, as I stood alone in that room I asked myself if I would be satisfied still to be in that position in 40 years time. In my heart I knew there was only one answer. The next step was to break the news to my parents. They were so happy that we were together again at home and they advised me to wait for three years in order to test the call. This I agreed to do.

Then began the process of appearing before Presbytery, and later the Candidates' Board; but in the meantime a kind friend who was a Greek scholar gave me free lessons in classical Greek for two years. Eventually I was faced with the entrance examination in Biblical knowledge and in Greek and when I appeared before the Board. I believe they had a sense of apprehension as my description of the call fell short of that which was expected. However, I came from a solid Welsh Calvinistic Methodist background and I was accepted. My home church was saddened rather than glad, possibly because of my increasing zeal.

The theological college was situated in a beautiful seaside town in West Wales. The buildings were imposing and the discipline required was acceptable to me. I wonder how many young men on entering theological college go through a kind of culture shock? The first revelations of higher criticism almost drove me to despair. Was there no more to the Christian faith than all these unreliable facts and uncertain truths? Amongst the students there was a group of fine men, about four in all, who stood out as different. They would meet frequently for prayer, and whenever I found myself in the company of one of them, although I felt a kind of kinship with them, there was a barrier between us. I had no idea what that barrier was until one of them challenged me about my faith. In my reply I listed all the good and commendable activities I was involved in, and when I had finished he very gently pointed out to me that I had been describing self-righteousness. By then I knew that I was not a Christian and it came as a terrible shock to me.

The first term came to an end and I talked to my parents about not returning to college. They responded by saying that the honourable thing to do was to return and complete the course, quoting the Biblical principle of perseverance. I loved my parents and felt greatly indebted to them. I would never consider going against their will, and so I returned. It is difficult to describe the deep chasm of conviction, a yearning for something that you could not explain. I felt as if there was a lost chord in my life that ruined every melody.

Then, one Saturday in January 1953, I experienced an upsetting incident. I had to leave for a village on the last bus to preach there the next day. When I alighted from the bus I met an elderly lady who kept what was called the chapel-house where I was to stay overnight. In conversation we began to talk about the Revival of 1904 which she remembered well and, to my astonishment, she informed me that it had meant nothing to her! I was deeply shocked that a person could be so near God's work and yet be untouched by it. As I spent the rest of that long evening alone, I knelt to pray and I was aware of a presence that I had not known before. In this glorious approach of God, I knew that I had become the Lord's and I praised and thanked Him for His mercy towards me. His truth became alive, and from then on there was no turning back.

The news that the Saviour was real had to be made known, and on returning to college I immediately and constantly challenged both staff and students. The good news of the Gospel was too glorious to be hidden and I honestly believed at that time that if you explained the way of salvation clearly to a person he or she would eagerly believe.

My college days came to an end and my first pastorate was in a mining town near Swansea. I had a branch church and also worked with the main church to which it was attached. Imagine having in your congregation the sister of Evan Roberts, the young man used of God in 1904. Her name was Mary Roberts and it was an inspiration to be in her company. Her husband was Sidney Evans who had been closely associated with Evan Roberts in those early days. As well as this, a lady called Miss Rachel Rees, who helped Evan Roberts spiritually before the Revival, attended the chapel. These and others soon became known to me and they often shared the vivid recollections that they had of better days.

My second pastorate was in the beautiful green hills of West Wales, in a village called Llanddewi-brefi, where my family spent four happy years. My wife, Morwen, whom I had met during my college days, knew far more of those very special people who had also been greatly blessed in 1904. We were partners together in the quest of seeking God in Revival power.

My third church was in Cardiff and is the one of which I am

presently the minister. When I first came here in 1962 I had only preached in English six times and I was more familiar with the Welsh Bible and hymns. Even so, there was no doubt in my mind that I was in God's will, and we both worked hard as we gave our all. After about two years I had a serious illness which was to remain with me for fifteen years. The first onset came with alarming suddenness and it was at that time, as I began to come to myself, that these words and phrases were formed in my mind. I cannot describe how near I felt to my Lord. Eventually I ventured to write them down:

> *"I saw a new vision of Jesus,*
> *A view I'd not seen here before,*
> *Beholding in glory so wondrous*
> *With beauty I had to adore.*
> *I stood on the shores of my weakness,*
> *And gazed at the brink of such fear;*
> *'Twas then that I saw Him in newness,*
> *Regarding Him fair and so dear."*

As I continued I realised that the lines had become a hymn. On my return home to my wife and three little children I felt so glad to be with them, yet I was reluctant to relinquish that living presence which I was then experiencing. The hymns remained silent for seven years, then I found a few more coming to me both in English and Welsh. Sometimes it would happen suddenly at night, and at such times I honestly felt as if I was a secretary writing them down. Not all came with such rapidity but many did, and my heart rejoiced in Him.

There is one hymn, however, that is perhaps the closest to my heart, and may be one that is more suitable for private meditation than public singing. It came at a time of great personal frailty and longing for God:

> *"Deep in my heart there is a sigh,*
> *A longing, Lord, for Thee;*
> *To know the depths that in Thee lie,*
> *The grace of Calvary.*

## Personal Testimony

*O grant that I might understand*
*Thy glorious mystery,*
*More of Thyself, and by Thy hand*
*Obedience stir in me. "*

Many others came in times of great joy and out of love that floods the heart. There have also been long periods of none, then followed a few more.

My hope is that these spiritual poems may in some small way help other travellers as we continue our journey home, fellow citizens of a great kingdom, the kingdom of God. We shall see the Lord Jesus Christ in all His majesty and be with God forever. For He is the end of the journey and the ultimate destination for us as Christians ... *"looking unto Jesus the author and finisher of our faith"* (Hebrews 12:2).

W. Vernon Higham
May 1998

# CONTENTS

# WORSHIP AND ADORATION

## 1

*Whom having not seen, ye love; in whom, though now ye see Him not, yet believing, ye rejoice with joy unspeakable and full of glory.*

I Peter 1:8

(77.77.D.  Aberystwyth *or* Hollingside)

Let my soul for ever praise
    What Thou art, O God above,
Worship Thee with joy, and raise
    Glorious anthems of Thy love.
Listen to my soul acclaim
    Wondrous stories of Thy care,
Thanking Thee for Him who came
    Ever more this joy to share.

Joy unspeakable is mine,
    Full of glory, full of grace,
Gift of mercy, love divine,
    Radiance of my Saviour's face!
Let this joy for ever flow,
    Till my being glows with Thee;
Let this radiance in me show
    Glimpses of eternity.

Who are these arrayed around,
    Breathing vengeance on my soul —
Fiery trials that surround,
    Testing hard if I am whole?
Yet my joy in Thee will stay;
    Knowing of Thy tenderness,
Nothing shall my heart dismay,
    Or remove Thy faithfulness.

Glorious joy, a gift from Thee
    Born in heaven, a child of grace,
Shows a gentleness to me
    With a smile from Thy dear face.
When I tremble in distress,
    And my heart cries out in pain,
Thou, my God, wilt ever bless,
    And this joy shall firm remain.

Then Thy ransomed shall be brought
    Unto Thine eternal fold,
Every soul that Thou hast bought,
    Fashioned, burnished in Thy mold.
Hear my heart rejoice in Thee;
    Overflowing grace abound;
Now and then my glory be,
    For in Christ my soul is found.

# 2

*For the Lord God is a sun and shield: the Lord will give grace and
glory: no good thing will He withhold from them that walk uprightly.*
Psalm 84:11

(77.77.D.  Hollingside *or* Aberystwyth)

See, my soul, the courts of God,
    Graced with mercy, peace and joy,
Where the saints have gladly trod,
    There to meet and Thee enjoy.
For Thy presence I will weep
    That I may in Thee delight;
Better far Thy doors to keep
    Than to dwell in sin's dark night.

## Worship and Adoration

Thou hast never failed Thine own,
    Strength to give upon life's race;
All their prayers before Thy throne
    Thou hast heard and granted grace.
Thou wilt never turn away,
    For I know Thy word of old;
Hear my cry and with me stay,
    That for Thee I may be bold.

Blest the days for him who lives
    In sweet fellowship with Thee;
Dark the seasons Satan gives,
    Souls to keep from Calvary.
To Thine altar bind my soul,
    Where Thy Son for sin has died;
Make my fainting spirit whole,
    O Thou glorious Crucified!

Nothing shall my soul now lack
    In the risen, living Lord;
Shield of faith from all attack
    And the thrusts of Satan's sword.
Jesus Christ, my Sun and Light,
    Is the joy my glad heart boasts;
O how amiable the sight
    Of the glorious Lord of hosts.

# 3

*Be thou faithful unto death, and I will give thee a crown of life.*

Revelation 2:10

(D.S.M.  Leominster)

Thanks be to Thee, my God,
   My heart and soul rejoice,
And praises blend in sweet accord
   In anthems of Thy choice.
O hear the gospel song,
   Our Saviour did atone,
With full forgiveness for my wrong,
   Saved by His grace alone.

Was ever grace like Thine
   Which always finds its own,
Is satisfied when Thou art mine,
   And turns me to Thy throne?
I'm saved by grace, I know,
   Embraced eternally
By arms of mercy here below,
   The folds of Calvary.

This confidence I bring
   That fears will all allay,
As tears of sorrow by this King
   Are gently wiped away.
I'll turn my gaze to see
   My risen glorious Lord,
And thank Him for the victory,
   The promise of His Word.

The end of faith He shows,
The fulness of His love,
And how He spares me from my foes
In bringing me above.
This is my home at last,
Where Jesus will me greet;
The crown He gives, I gladly cast
Beneath His feet.

# 4

*God be merciful to me a sinner.*

Luke 18:13

(76.76.D.  Penlan)

Far off I see the kindness
And beauty of Thy face;
Yet tremble at such firmness,
But thank Thee for Thy grace.
The stars in all their glory
Can never Thee outshine,
For they are but a memory
Upon the map of time.

Thou art the Lord Almighty,
Creator, Sovereign King,
Omnipotent and holy;
Thy grace my heart will sing.
For men, with all their power
And pride in human birth,
Are but a fading flower
Upon the field of earth.

## Worship and Adoration

Yet all are Thy creation
    And made for Thy delight;
The precious word salvation
    Now dawns upon my sight.
The Son of God the Father,
    With love and tender care,
Has shown the greatest wonder
    Of gospel truth so fair.

My only name is sinner;
    I have no right to plead,
No merit to consider;
    I failed Thy word to heed.
I tremble as Thy mercy
    Unfolds new hope to me,
And call for this great pity,
    And gaze at Calvary.

The Saviour stands in glory,
    But, O my soul, behold
That blood, those wounds so costly,
    When Jesus Christ was sold.
He died a ransom payment
    For sinners such as I;
Now see my great enjoyment,
    For God has heard my cry.

# 5

*Bless the Lord, O my soul: and all that is within me,*
*bless His holy name.*

Psalm 103:1

(D.C.M.  Ellacombe)

O let my lips sing forth Thy praise,
    Thy majesty adore;
And grant this heart of mine to raise
    Sweet songs for evermore.
For Thou art King, head over all;
    Creation in Thy palm;
Thy sovereign will, with might can call
    The storm of time to calm.

In mists beyond our furthest thought,
    Thy power is still supreme;
And by Thy Word alone, from nought
    Springs forth a flowing stream.
Yet here am I upon this earth,
    With mortal frame and weak;
My angry passions blinding me,
    Lest I my Lord should seek.

I thank Thee for constraining grace
    Which drew my soul to Thee,
And from the depths of sin's disgrace,
    At last I to Thee flee.
The blood of Jesus Christ alone
    Removes my guilty stains;
I stand redeemed for Thou hast borne
    The might of sin and pain.

# 6

*Bless the Lord, O my soul: and all that is within me,*
*bless His holy name.*

Psalm 103:1

(664.666.4.  Malvern)

My soul will ever praise,
My heart an anthem raise,
　To bless the Lord.
Glory shall fill the sky,
For God Himself is nigh,
He gladly hears my cry
　With sweet accord.

Brief is my span of life,
Shadowed by sin and strife;
　Death will not stay.
Like unto flowers of grass,
Sadly my fame will pass;
All that I am, alas,
　Will fade away!

Blessings abound to me,
Thy kindness covers me,
　O God of grace!
All my unworthiness,
Thou hast removed no less
Than distant East and West,
　By Thine embrace.

Angels and men acclaim
Glorious Son who came
　To make me whole!
My soul is washed, with those
Whom God the Father chose,
When Christ did interpose,
　And saved my soul!

# 7

*Which hope we have as an anchor of the soul,*
*both sure and steadfast, and which entereth into that within the veil.*

Hebrews 6:19

(64.64.66.64. Tryst)

Wonderful truth unfold
    Grace to declare;
Beautiful words now told
    Mercy doth bear.
Thou art adorable,
Thy grace unchangeable,
Thy word immutable,
    Beyond compare.

Where shall my soul recline,
    Except in Thee?
How shall this heart of mine
    Find Calvary?
Take my unrighteousness
In Thy great tenderness;
Remove my foolishness;
    This is my plea.

Then in tempestuous sea,
    In storm or gale,
If I forgotten be,
    Thou wilt prevail.
Anchor my soul to Thee,
Fastened to Calvary,
Holding eternally,
    Never to fail.

Worship and Adoration

Then I shall enter in
Drawn by Thy grace,
When all are gathered in
To see Thy face.
Now to adore Thy name,
Discarding all my shame,
Grant me a living frame,
Thee to embrace.

# 8

*Glory to God in the highest, and on earth peace, good will toward men.*
Luke 2:14

(66.84.D.  Leoni *or* Dolwyddelan)

All glory to our God
Who dwells in light sublime;
His sceptre is a sparkling rod,
With power divine.
Behold His mercy-seat,
A throne of grace and peace;
His face of love and passion sweet
From fears release.

Creation is His plan,
A beauteous whole;
And from the dust, He formed a man,
A living soul.
Before man fell His grace
Reached out with hand outspread;
Then Jesus moved our sin's disgrace,
And Satan fled.

## Worship and Adoration

The angels anthems sing,
And shepherds gladly call,
As wise men costly gifts now bring
To infant small.
Our souls cry out the song:
'Glory to God on high';
We praise His name, embrace His love:
He brought us nigh.

The host in heaven above
Join with the saints below
To worship now our God of love,
His glories show.
O Father, Spirit, Son,
O blessèd Union thrice,
We fall before the Holy One,
The Pearl of price.

# 9

*Our Saviour Jesus Christ, who hath abolished death,*
*and hath brought life and immortality to light through the gospel.*

2 Timothy 1:10

(65.65.66.65. Moab)

O Saviour of my soul
Let me adore Thee,
When life has left its toll,
And I am empty.
It is Thy hand of love
That lifts me far above:
O blessèd Holy Dove,
Who shows me glory!

## Worship and Adoration

Christ hath abolished death,
 O conquest glorious,
Through life of living breath,
 My King victorious.
For Thou hast brought to light
Immortal life so bright,
That I may claim the sight
 Of heights so wondrous!

O blessèd soul that lies
 Within redemption;
Reposes and relies
 In safe salvation.
O happy my estate,
Where grace does not abate;
Then enter through that gate
 Of full salvation.

Then to behold Thy face
 Of peace and beauty,
Forever Thee embrace,
 O Lord of mercy.
Then shall I know as known
And love my Lord's renown,
Thy majesty to crown,
 O King of glory.

# 10

*I waited patiently for the Lord;*
*and he inclined unto me, and heard my cry.*

Psalm 40:1

(86.86.88.88.  Moriah)

Let my soul now praise the Saviour,
Sent by God and sped by love;
With a will that would not waver,
To perfect His plan of love.

*From the pit of death He called me,*
*Quickened me by grace divine:*
*Brightness of His Father's glory,*
*Image strong in me to shine.*

Jesus is the name we cherish,
Of the Christ of God alone;
He has promised none shall perish
Who receive Him as His own.

Who can fathom founts of mercy,
Found in depths of costly grace?
Flood of pardon poured in plenty
As He took the sinner's place.

Not in heaven, not in glory
Shall we measure, measureless;
Yet to know and know it fully,
He could never love us less.

This is love within the Godhead,
Pure and perfect, all divine;
Passion pales with joy exalted,
Christ the Saviour now is mine.

# 11

*Who shall lay anything to the charge of God's elect?*

Romans 8:33

(D.C.M. St. Matthew)

We stand before the Judge of time,
  His throne a place of fear;
And gaze upon the King sublime,
  With trembling hearts draw near.
But none can charge the elect of Christ
  With lies and wickedness,
There richly robed, surpassing price,
  Imputed righteousness.

Secure the bonds of blessedness
  On Calvary wrought with love;
No famine, sword or nakedness,
  Can make our faith remove.
For who can separate the saint
  When links are forged by Him,
Who chose His path without complaint,
  And bore the weight of sin?

No space beyond, no scheme or plan,
  No circumstance can change;
For present past and future span
  Are in His sovereign range.
His grace persuades and tells my heart,
  That conqueror I shall be;
From sin and death and judgement's dart,
  Secure eternally.

## The Triune God

The love of Christ is vast and deep,
  No measurement can tell;
His sacrifice our death-like sleep
  Will evermore dispel.
If we are killed or we are torn
  With persecution's hate,
We never, never are forlorn —
  We are regenerate.

Predestined from the depths divine,
  Deep in the will of God;
Displayed in time, of David's line,
  This earth a Saviour trod.
He bled and died for sin and shame,
  And rose to justify;
His majesty is all our fame,
  Our Christ we glorify.

# 12

*For day and night Thy hand was heavy upon me.*

Psalm 32:4

(87.87.887.  Dies Irae *or* Elberfeld)

Thy living word my heart did break
  When I beheld the Saviour;
From paths of sorrow I did wake
  To seek Thy mighty favour.
Mercy of God, atoning love,
Spirit of joy, flow from above,
  Thy gentle grace revealing.

Thy searching eye exposed my sin
  And motives so unworthy;
Shame and remorse now welled within;
  Thy gaze was full of pity.

### The Triune God

Mercy of God disturbing me,
Spirit of truth and purity,
   Thy gentle grace revealing.

Thy loving hand restrained my way,
   In righteousness to follow;
Thy will prevailed lest I should stray,
   And cause my soul to sorrow.
Mercy of God, constraining care,
Spirit of light beyond compare,
   Thy gentle grace revealing.

Thy tender dealing with my heart,
   Most painful, yet with healing;
This grace that bids me not depart,
   Pours balm with love constraining.
Mercy of God, eternal, strong,
Spirit of grace with victor's song,
   Thy gentle grace revealing.

# 13

*And there shall in no wise enter into it any thing that defileth,*
*neither whatsoever worketh abomination, or maketh a lie:*
*but they which are written in the Lamb's book of life.*

Revelation 21:27

(D.S.M.  Llanllyfni)

I heard the Father's cry,
   Who turns away from sin:
He shuts the gates, and those who try
   Can never enter in.
Then heaven is barred to me,
   My fancied merit, loss:
My woeful lot — where can I flee
   And rid my soul of dross?

## The Triune God

How shall I find a way
    To come to God above;
When all my efforts lead astray,
    My poor soul pants for love?
'Tis then I see His grace,
    Revealing mercy's part;
Then all my sin and life's disgrace
    I lay on Jesus' heart.

O Saviour now so kind,
    What heart of love is Thine!
For all my sin and stain I find
    On Christ the King divine.
What can I say, my Lord?
    What tongue can ever tell?
The gift of grace does now afford
    A path that passes hell.

My Saviour's merit pleads
    A place for me to stand;
An advocate who intercedes;
    My Hope, at God's right hand.
Who is this Friend I need,
    Who shed His blood for me?
Behold the Christ, whose death and deed
    Forgive eternally!

What does He show to God
    That satisfies His heart,
That stems His wrath, and stays His rod,
    And bids me not depart?
It is His righteousness,
    Displayed in Christ His Son,
Has granted me this blessedness,
    That Christ alone has won.

## The Triune God

Then I shall praise His name
  With songs that come from Him;
He granted me a heart aflame
  That sin can never dim.
Rejoice, my soul, rejoice!
  O glorious Trinity,
My cup is full, and fills my voice
  With gratitude to Thee.

# 14

*Looking unto Jesus the author and finisher of our faith.*

Hebrews 12:2

(L.M.  Eden)

O glorious God, so full of grace,
  Wonderful joy is Thine embrace.
We worship Thee with pure delight,
  Thou art our Father, wondrous sight.

We bless Thy name for mercy fair,
  As we behold Thy heart of care;
For Thou hast planned a way supreme,
  An act of mercy, glorious theme!

Behold the mercy of the Son!
  With eager heart He came, to run
The race proclaimed by heaven above,
  A path of grace, a crown of love.

O! bitter pain, both sweet and good,
  The piercing nails, the hardy wood.
Thou blest Redeemer, laurels fine
  Hast won for me, a feat divine.

## The Triune God

Eternal Spirit, Fount of fire,
　　With tender swiftness, truth, inspire
The heart of man, in sin of earth,
　　To lift him from the power of death.

O blessèd Sword and Shaft of light,
　　Dispel the darkness of our night;
And shed the glory of the Lord,
　　With song of sweet delight and chord.

Ethereal praises ring the skies,
　　Celestial hymns of heaven rise;
On earth, with bliss of praise below,
　　We join the anthem as we bow.

To God the Father, blessèd Christ,
　　The Holy Ghost, blest Union Thrice,
The Triune God, and God alone
　　Be praise and worship at the throne.

# 15

*I pray for them: I pray not for the world, but for them which Thou hast given me;*
*for they are Thine. And all Mine are Thine, and Thine are Mine;*
*and I am glorified in them.*

John 17:9,10

(77.77.D. Hollingside *or* Aberystwyth)

God eternal, can it be,
　　From beyond the clouds of time,
Thou hast chosen even me,
　　Named me in Thy courts sublime?
Timeless grace, immortal love
　　Now in Christ has filled my soul,
With this knowledge from above,
　　That He took sin's heavy toll.

## The Triune God

Though I search, I cannot bring
    Any merit that will gain;
Tarnished, tainted, every thing
    Sin has touched, my spirit slain.
Was it, Lord, to such as I,
    Deep in sin's depravity,
That Thy mercy called to fly
    Out of darkness unto Thee?

Chosen by Thy grace alone,
    Hidden reasons to Thee known;
All I know, Thou didst atone,
    Claimed and took me as Thine own.
Chosen Saviour to redeem,
    Costly mission to perform,
Work peculiar, yet supreme,
    As He took our human form.

Thine I am, Thy prayer reveals,
    For the Father brought me nigh;
Such security appeals
    That Thy truth will sanctify.
Even me, how can it be
    That these lips should sing Thy praise?
Sweet Redeemer, now I see
    What it costs to grant this grace.

# 16

*As for God, His way is perfect.*
Psalm 18:30
(D.C.M. Ellacombe)

Thy perfect law is my delight,
    O Lord of truth and grace;
In all Thy ways a beauteous sight
    To aid us in our race.
To love the Lord my God above,
    My neighbour as my own,
Is Thy command, O Lord of love,
    Thy Spirit now has shown.

Thy perfect law now dwells within
    And whispers peace to me;
The breath of pardon for my sin
    Thy pain at Calvary.
O may this love now richly flow,
    And grant me sweet increase;
Thus let my heart forever know
    The touch of heaven's peace.

Thy perfect name a melody
    Of grace I will endear;
Yet Satan fears and devils flee
    The name they dread to hear.
Now in my heart He is my King,
    My Sovereign Lord of all;
I humbly bow and gladly sing —
    'Tis fragrance to my soul.

# 17

*In whom we have redemption through His blood,*
*the forgiveness of sins according to the riches of His grace.*

Ephesians 1:7

(86.886.  Newcastle)

O Father, Son and Holy Dove,
　　The radiance of Thy face
Outshines the stars in heaven above
With costly smile of Calvary's love,
　　The riches of Thy grace.

Amongst the sons of men on earth
　　To Thee belongs all fame;
For Thou hast granted lasting worth,
And touched our souls with wondrous birth:
　　All glory to Thy name!

In times of turmoil and dismay,
　　When Satan does release
His anger vile in evil sway,
Thy strength is all I need each day,
　　The beauty of Thy peace.

I worship Thee who reigns supreme,
　　I bathe in mercy mild;
My guilt removed, O glorious theme,
Far, far above my sweetest dream,
　　Now found in Bethlehem's child.

# 18

*Whom having not seen, ye love; in whom, though now ye see him not, yet*
*believing, ye rejoice with joy unspeakable and full of glory.*

1 Peter 1:8

(10.10.10.10.  Toulon)

Author of life and fount of truth and grace,
Source of all being, grant my soul a place.
Thou Rose of Sharon, fairest of my heart
Whisper assurance that can ne'er depart.

Spirit of Christ, and Comforter, I greet,
Speak to my soul Thy confirmation sweet;
Spirit to spirit, seal my heart to Thine,
In marks of grace that make Thee ever mine.

When I despair upon life's weary way,
Grant Abba, Father, Thou wilt with me stay,
Never to leave me, always be my guide,
Keeping me close to Thy Son's piercèd side.

I have not seen Thee with my naked eye,
Yet I believe the God that cannot lie;
I have not seen Thee, yet I love Thy Name,
Unspeakable my joy, my heart aflame!

Blessèd inheritance to me belong,
O how my soul thrills with salvation's song:
Thanks be to God for all Thou dost provide;
Glory to Thee in whom I now abide.

# 19

Based on 1 Peter 1.

(D.C.M. Rhos)

Grant me a glimpse of glory Lord
  Upon my pilgrimage;
A deep assurance from Thy Word,
  Make precious every page.
'O glory in the highest' sing
  To Thy almighty name;
The end of faith declare, my King,
  Inspire my hope to flame.

There is a place of peace and joy,
  Inheritance of God,
Where I shall all my praise employ
  To magnify the Lord.
There is a place of purity,
  Corruption cannot spoil,
A home reserved in heaven for me,
  The end of all my toil.

This precious faith more fine than gold
  Is fiercely tried by fire,
But Thou wilt never lose Thy hold
  Nor fail in moments dire.
He glorifies His name in me,
  His honour to declare;
In ways of wisest mystery
  He guides my soul with care.

With joy unspeakable my heart
  Lays hold on God above;
The knowledge that I have a part
  Tells me of His great love.

## The Triune God

O speak to me in accents clear,
    And tell me I am Thine;
O tell me, show me, I am dear,
    Close to Thy heart divine.

Invisible to human eye,
    I have not seen my Lord,
Yet with a heart of faith I cry,
    I love Thee O my God.
This living hope of life is mine;
    Thy love shed in my heart;
The God of grace and peace will shine
    Within me, ne'er to part.

My eyes shall see Thy blessèd face
    In God's eternal rest,
When I have run Thy chosen race,
    Rejoicing with the blest.
O then shall I Thy face behold
    With unbeclouded sight,
A ransomed soul within Thy fold,
    A child of God's delight.

# 20

Based on Psalm 80.

(D.C.M. Ladywell)

Visit this vine, O Lord most high,
    Thy people claim as Thine;
O hear our cry and come Thou nigh,
    Thy church in sad decline.
Have mercy, Lord, upon Thine own,
    This vineyard of Thy choice;
O hearken to her gracious groan
    And let her hear Thy voice.

# The Triune God

Thy voice, O Lord, that called the earth,
  The sun and stars to be;
O speak to us, dispel this dearth
  With glorious remedy.
Thy church that once in faithfulness
  Set our dear land aflame;
The heathen mock in foolishness
  The honour of Thy name.

O look upon this vine again,
  And see her barrenness;
O grant that those that her disdain
  Shall cause no more distress.
O call upon the Son of Man,
  Inspire Thy quickening Word,
To heal Thy vineyard by the One
  On Thy right hand, our Lord.

Triumphant Zion now proclaim
  The glory of Thy grace;
Restore Thy vine, remove her shame,
  Reveal to her Thy face.
Thy holy presence grant this vine,
  And quicken her again
With life abundant, power divine;
  Lord now forever reign!

# 21

*For we know that if our earthly house of this tabernacle were dissolved, we have a building of God, an house not made with hands, eternal in the heavens.*

2 Corinthians 5:1

(S.M.  Sarah)

The God of grace and love,
　　Who holds me to His breast:
My present peace, my home above
　　In His protection rest.

But for a moment brief
　　Sorrows surround my days;
Yet with a glorious glad belief
　　I see my hope and stay.

Exceeding is the weight
　　Of glory for the saint;
Surpassing thought, celestial sight
　　For those who will not faint.

I have a mansion fair,
　　A home not made by hand,
A place prepared with holy care,
　　Designed by His command.

Whilst in this body worn,
　　My spirit groans for Thee;
Yet in my heart a hope is born —
　　Immortal I shall be.

Then shall I praise His name,
　　Sweet melody of grace;
Fashioned anew, in glorious frame,
　　I shall behold His face.

# GOD THE FATHER

# 22

*And in that day thou shalt say, O Lord, I will praise Thee:*
*though Thou wast angry with me, Thine anger is turned away,*
*and Thou comfortedst me.*

Isaiah 12: 1

(77.77.D.  Aberystwyth)

Lord Almighty, King Divine,
    Thou who knowest all mankind,
Gazed upon this life of mine,
    Satisfaction could not find.
Yet Thine anger turned away,
    Undeserving mercy flowed;
And Thy comfort was my stay,
    When I saw Thy love unfold.

Love immense and love so sweet,
    Love beyond my dearest dream;
Love that gives, this love I greet,
    For it flows an endless stream.
Such a fount is God alone,
    Source of all His saving wealth;
Christ alone does now atone,
    Died and rose to give us health.

Here I'll trust, and will not fear,
    In Jehovah, God supreme;
Strong in heart with song endear;
    Hear my praises and redeem.
From this wealth salvation flows,
    He will always meet my needs;
Praise His name, my longing knows,
    As I drink, my soul He feeds.

# 23

*But we have this treasure in earthen vessels,*
*that the excellency of the power may be of God, and not of us.*

2 Corinthians 4:7

(86.886.  Rest)

O God supreme, we Thee adore,
   Thy sovereign scope behold:
The powers of darkness did abhor,
But failed to meet Thy mighty store
   Of strength and power untold.

The truth of God will never fade,
   The source of light and peace:
At His command the worlds were made,
And glorious gospel to our aid
   Thy mercy did release.

A humble soul of brokenness
   Thou never wilt despise:
For mercy dwells and gentleness
Within Thy heart of tenderness;
   Contrition Thou dost prize.

O God of grace, my heart did win
   A treasure come from Thee:
My vessel frail, but Christ within;
Lord, break my heart, forgive my sin,
   And show Thyself in me.

The knowledge of the Lord of light
   Is shed within my heart:
A mind illuminated bright
Beholds salvation with new sight;
   Now sin and death depart.

# 24

*According as He hath chosen us in Him before the foundation of the world,*
*that we should be holy and without blame before Him in love.*

Ephesians 1:4

(D.L.M.  Merthyr Tydfil *or* Peterborough)

O glorious Majesty on high,
    Eternal splendour is Thy dress,
Where seraphims for ever fly,
    With songs of sweetest holiness.
Beyond the confines of our mind,
    In realms outreaching human sight,
In perfect blessedness we find,
    By faith, Thy glorious image bright.

The joy of truth shines in Thy face,
    Of sovereign grace and mercy's smile;
And in the bosom of Thy grace
    Election cradled without guile.
Thy perfect will becomes our joy
    When we have seen Thy heart of love;
Our eager lips we now employ
    To sing the praise of God above.

Thy perfect plan for all Thine own
    Is born in every chosen heart;
Forbid it then that we should roam,
    Or ever seek from Thee to part.
To Thee predestined to conform,
    And bear Thine image in our lives,
With glorious gown and shining crown, —
    And all this from Thy grace derives!

God the Father

Who brings this grace unto the dead,
   With quickening life and serious call?
It is the Saviour who has led
   A host of souls since Adam's fall.
With costly merit, pardon pure,
   He has redeemed His chosen flock;
The faith He gives will now endure,
   And stand forever on this Rock.


# 25

*How long, Lord? wilt Thou hide Thyself for ever?*
*shall Thy wrath burn like fire?*

Psalm 89:46

(L.M.  Duke Street)


The ways of God outspan the sky,
   His word will make the tempest cry;
His glorious realms outreach my thought,
   And show me daily I am nought.

My glorious God is judgement's seat,
   And mercy flows with love complete
From God to me, this love divine
   Embraces all this need of mine.

My wilful pride raised up its head,
   And sought to guide my feet, instead
Of God alone, who is my King
   And Righteousness, of whom I sing.

For, hidden in the heart divine
   Is wrath and holiness sublime;
It purges hard, it washes clean,
   And on His arm it makes me lean.

## God the Father

The enemies of truth delight
To see the saints in dismal plight;
They cry in glee their end to see
And tremble not, as needs must be.

How long, O Lord, Thy love withhold?
How long Thine anger, grief untold?
My mortal shame the wretch I am,
My shortened youth at Thy command.

Sweet covenant of God, whose plan
Of grace distils the soul of man;
My heart is pure, I know I'm Thine,
My confidence on Thee recline.

Thy former truths unchanging still,
Thy love and mercy are my fill,
Thy stern rebuke, or chastening sweet
I'll trust Thee all my needs to meet.

My Lord and God is King of all,
He guides my footsteps lest I fall;
Praise loud His name, His mercy sing:
The Lord Omnipotent is King.

For ever true the immortal throne,
The Triune God, yet He alone
Extends His covenant to men,
The blood of Christ and heaven's Amen.

God the Father

# 26

*Who shall ascend into the hill of the Lord? or who shall stand in His holy place?*
*He that hath clean hands, and a pure heart; who hath not lifted up his soul unto*
*vanity, nor sworn deceitfully.*

Psalm 24:3,4

(86.86.88.  Tydi a Roddaist)

The Lord of glory formed the earth
    And all that dwell therein;
His ancient power of life gave birth
    To hope, for those in sin.
For who shall climb this mount of grace,
Or ever stand in that pure place?

The King of glory opened wide
    The gates of truth and love;
His hands and heart and wounded side
    Were heaven's delight above.
For who shall climb this mount of grace,
Or ever stand in that pure place?

The God of glory pardon gives
    To those with hearts that seek;
A generation blessed, that lives
    To hear the gospel speak.
For who shall climb this mount of grace,
Or ever stand in that pure place?

For these are they who stand one day
    Before Thy throne of grace,
With hands and hearts and lips that say,
    'Behold His lovely face.'
The mount of grace shall now rejoice,
And glory ever be its choice.

## God the Father

The gates of heaven are lifted high,
  And hallelujahs ring;
The ransomed hearts of sinners cry
  'Hosanna,' to their King!
For these are they that stand in joy,
And all their praises now employ.

Amen, amen, amen.

# 27

*In all these things we are more than conquerors
through Him that loved us.*

Romans 8:37

(D.C.M.  Vox Dilecti)

There is a fount of costly love
  Found in Thy heart sublime;
Redemption planned in heaven above,
  Fulfilled by Thee in time.
This painful sacrifice of grace,
  With message that He died,
Brings to my soul the smiling face
  Of justice satisfied.

There is a gentleness of peace
  Around Thy throne divine;
A place where grace will now release
  The flow of mercy's wine.
The peace of God is vast and pure,
  No words can ever tell;
It cannot fail, it will endure,
  Withstand the gates of hell.

## God the Father

There is a power of strength untold
 That comes from Thee alone,
Which gives me courage, makes me bold,
 Transforms my heart of stone.
I am persuaded now at last,
 When I behold Thy care,
That I am safe from Satan's blast:
 No more shall I despair.

In every thing and every place,
 In every changing wind,
I'll trust in Thee along life's race,
 And find Thee to be kind.
Thou liftest me by Thy great hand,
 By many foes oppressed;
As more than conqueror I stand:
 The victory of the blessed.

# 28

*And I saw a great white throne, and him that sat on it,
from whose face the earth and the heaven fled away;
and there was found no place for them.*

Revelation 20:11

(88.88.88. St. Catherine)

What wondrous sight now fills the skies,
 The terror of the Lord displayed?
The final breath of time now dies,
 And all the scenes of life are played;
The sea gives up its ancient dead,
And shrill the call of trumpet dread.

## God the Father

Sad lake, its waters full of gall,
    Within its depths the second death;
I saw the dead both great and small,
    Before the God of life and breath,
With book of doom condemning men,
And book of life, the grace of heaven.

O God of love and justice pure,
    Cover my soul with righteousness;
Send to my heart the wondrous cure,
    Thy precious blood and cleansing dress,
That I may stand in bold array,
And sing with joy on Judgement Day.

# 29

*To him that overcometh will I give to eat of the tree of life,*
*which is in the midst of the paradise of God.*

Revelation 2:7

(8.10.10.4.  Ellasgarth)

Eternal God, O sovereign grace,
    Glory is Thine in all Thou dost decree.
Grace flowed in floods of sorrow and of grief:
    By love set free.

Creation crowned, out of the dust,
    Eden man's home and all for him to reign;
Fair flower of innocence was crushed and soiled:
    To Thee such pain.

Voice of the Lord, echoed in vain,
    Sad was the garden in the cool of day.
Where art thou man, the image of Myself?
    So far away!

## God the Father

Paradise lost, O tragic fall!
   Sin now imprisoned man in hell's firm hold;
Satan held sway and ruled in might on earth,
   With wiles so bold.

Never was grief, like unto Thine:
   Bitter the cup in sad Gethsemane,
Heavy the cross and harsh the crown of thorns;
   O Calvary!

Never was love, like unto Thine:
   Sinless and pure He took our place of shame;
Lonely the cry forsaken and forlorn:
   His love aflame.

Never was joy, like unto Thine:
   Death crushed in dust by resurrection might;
Paradise gained for sinners found in Him;
   O glorious sight!

# 30

Based on Revelation 7.

(87.87.47.  Price)

Lift my gaze, O Lord Almighty,
   To behold Thee face to face:
Robed in Christ in purest beauty,
   Stand before the throne of grace.
   Thy Redemption
Found for me with Thee a place.

## God the Father

God Himself draws ever nearer,
  Dries my tears with tender care;
Sorrow's vale no more can sever,
  None can challenge Him or dare.
    Safely cradled
  In the arms of grace so fair.

Long my hungry soul hath sought Thee,
  Faltered, failed and bowed my head;
Then at last Thy voice has bid me
  Feast upon the living bread.
    Satisfaction,
  To that soul by Thee is fed.

In this fallen sad creation
  Grief and anguish often reign;
Yet the suffering of salvation,
  He alone could bear the pain
    Of our pardon:
  He alone for sin was slain.

Burdened with a weight of sorrow
  Thou hast laid my heart so low;
Yet God lifts my soul to follow,
  Cast my burden in love's flow,
    Fills my vessel,
  With a joy Thy children know.

Deep within my heart confusion,
  Thou hast heard my cry for rest;
Troubled by the storms of passion,
  And the tempest of my breast.
    Thou hast heard me,
  Loved and granted my request.

## God the Father

Who are these Thy grace delights in?
  What their story, whence they came?
These are they afflicted for Thee,
  Loved Thy Gospel, braved the flame.
    Righteous children,
    Robed in white, acclaim Thy fame.

Come, O Christ, in all Thy splendour,
  Claim Thy children for Thine own;
Mansions fair display Thy favour,
  Manifest Thy great renown.
    Resurrection,
    Robed immortal, glorious gown.

In the Gospel of salvation
  All these sorrows are no more;
Now we face a new creation,
  Endless joys await in store.
    Heirs of glory
    Enter now through Christ the door.

# GOD THE SON

# 31

*O death where is Thy sting? O grave, where is thy victory?*

1 Corinthians 15:55

(66.84.D.  Dolwyddelan)

See Christ the Victor raised
In resurrection life,
The mighty arm of God displayed,
Who ends the strife.
He is the Lord of all,
Whose arm is shortened not;
See devils' flight, and Satan's fall,
And hell their lot.

What miracle of grace
To mortal life's brief span,
So marred by sin and hell's disgrace,
A glorious plan!
The Father on me looked,
And saw my great distress;
He wove a gown, He only could,
Immortal dress.

The sting of death is sin,
The power of law declares;
But Jesus Christ the Son doth win —
Our guilt He bears.
Behold, ye sinners, now,
And look to Christ alone;
Behold the blood upon His brow —
He did atone.

## God the Son

Be steadfast in life's race,
  Abounding in His way,
For all we do is by His grace,
    For we would stray.
  He took mortality
  With sin's corrupting blight,
And nailed it all to Calvary's tree,
    To give us light.

  Immortal is my dress,
    Corruption fled away;
Now robed in Him, yes, nothing less,
    In bright array.
  O death, where is thy sting?
  O grave, thy victory?
The living Christ on mercy's wing
    Grants peace to me.


# 32

*I find in him no fault at all.*

John 18:38

(64.64.66.64.  Something for Thee)

  See yonder Calvary,
    Crowned with a cross;
  God's mercy now declares
    Sin's final loss.
  Justice and mercy meet,
  Love at the Saviour's feet;
  Gentle the grace we greet,
    Pardon so sweet.

## God the Son

Here is my radiant Lord,
   Sin cannot dim;
Look on His lovely life,
   No guilt in Him.
Though men did spit and scorn,
Spurned Him and truth have torn,
See God in human form,
   Christ virgin-born.

What woeful, foul abyss
   Startles my soul?
What weary load I bear,
   Sin's heavy toll!
O Blessèd Trinity,
Thrice Holy Unity:
Gaze on His purity,
   No guilt in Thee.

Lord, I shall never cross,
   Sad is my lot;
Jordan shall on me roll,
   Strength I have not.
Yet a great sight I see,
My sin is nailed on Thee;
Grant grace eternally,
   No guilt in me.

Strange and amazing truth,
   Hope lights my heart:
God in His mercy stooped,
   Love to impart.
See how my soul will soar,
Faith leads me to the store,
Gone all the guilt of yore —
   Grace evermore!

# 33

*When he is come, he will reprove the world of sin,*
*and of righteousness, and of judgement.*

John 16:8

(86.84.  St. Cuthbert)

O Sacred Breath and Holy One
    Who whispers truth to me,
I thank Thee for Thy blessèd dawn,
    At Calvary.

'Twas by the power of clarity
    My shame came to the light,
Showed depths of my depravity —
    My sinful plight.

Amazing tenderness of grace
    Exposing my estate,
With more in view than my disgrace —
    No taunt of hate.

My wild alarm is turned away
    When gently led by Thee;
My gaze is fixed on that pure ray
    Of hope for me.

O perfect love that robed the cross
    With grace of heaven's birth;
An act in time to Satan's loss,
    Eternal worth.

O tender Spirit, by whose acts
    Sweet pain was brought to me;
My happy spirit flies through tracts
    Of bliss so free.

## God the Son

A light now shines within my heart
No terror dark dispels,
For Christ my Lord will not depart:
His Spirit dwells.

And I shall join that throng above
Who sing of Calvary,
Of God eternal and of Love —
O Blessèd Three!

# 34

*And you hath He quickened, who were dead in trespasses and sins.*

Ephesians 2:1

(88.88.88. Pater Omnium)

Author of life and pardoning love,
We thank Thee for Thy Holy Dove,
Sweet visitant of grace and light,
Whose quickening touch dispelled my night;
The blood of Christ absolved my stain,
And brought me near to God again.

At Calvary's cross I saw His face,
And stood amazed at truth and grace:
My vain good work and life of pride
Stood now exposed at His dear side;
O heavy punishment so dread!
He took it all for me instead.

What does this mean, the dead alive?
For none but God could e'er contrive
A scheme devised in realms sublime,
And penetrating into time —
This sinful man, incapable,
Quickened by God adorable!

## God the Son

Wonderful Saviour from above
Livened my soul, imparting love;
Called from the dead to live with Thee
On earth, and then eternally.
Praises and joy now fill my soul,
For Thou art Lord, my all in all.

# 35

*After this, Jesus knowing that all things were now accomplished,*
*that the scripture might be fulfilled, saith, I thirst.*

John 19:28

(D.C.M.  Rhos)

I heard the cry of mercy mild
    Which broke my heart in two:
A voice so full for me His child —
    My soul towards Him flew.
'I thirst', He cried with parching heart,
    'Forgive them', was His song;
And heaven heard and hell did start,
    For He had done no wrong.

No sponge of wine with bitter stain
    His thirst could ever quench:
The ocean wide and clouds of rain
    This desert never drench.
For souls He called, for hearts He pined,
    This satisfaction strange:
He cried for me, and showed mankind
    The love that does not change.

His thirsty soul He satisfied,
    And called me by His Name.
He drew me close to His dear side
    And told me why He came:

## God the Son

The eternal plan of God for man
    Fulfilled on painful tree;
His blood was shed, and showed the span
    Of love so wide and free.

Beyond the cross and bitter curse,
    I see God's plan sublime:
He breaks the clouds of death for us —
    Pours mercy into time.
Was ever agony like this,
    That spread such life abroad?
For at the cross see mercy's kiss
    Which drew us to the Lord.

# 36

*And when He was come into Jerusalem,*
*all the city was moved, saying, Who is this?*
Matthew 21:10

(87.87.47.  Bryn Calfaria)

Who is this with joy approaching
    Happy men who see His face?
'Tis the Saviour, healing, speaking,
    Full of truth and full of grace.
        Son of David,
    Grant me sight, and Thine embrace.

Who is this, with men acclaiming,
    Born the Son of David's line,
Hallelujahs, palm leaves waving?
    'Tis the Christ, the Son Divine.
        Loud Hosannas!
    Come, O Lord, for Thee we pine.

### God the Son

Who is this, on cross so lonely,
    Hanging there for men to see?
'Tis the Lord of all the glory,
    Bearing penalty for me.
        O forgive me!
Plead my cause eternally.

Who is this in glory standing,
    Victor over death and shame,
Risen glorious, ever pleading?
    'Tis a sweet and wondrous Name!
        Blessèd Jesus!
Praise the Lord who took my blame!

# 37

*Great is the mystery of godliness:*
1 Timothy 3:16
(10 10. 10 10.  Pantyfedwyn)

Great is the gospel of our glorious God,
Where mercy met the anger of God's rod;
A penalty was paid and pardon bought,
And sinners lost, at last to Him were brought:

    *O let the praises of my heart be Thine,*
    *For Christ has died that I may call Him mine,*
    *That I may sing with those who dwell above,*
    *Adoring, praising Jesus, King of Love.*

Great is the mystery of godliness,
Great is the work of God's own holiness;
It moves my soul, and causes me to long
For greater joys than to the earth belong:

God the Son

The Spirit vindicated Christ our Lord,
And angels sang with joy and sweet accord;
The nations heard, a dark world flamed with light —
When Jesus rose in glory and in might:

# 38

*But God commendeth His love towards us, in that,
while we were yet sinners, Christ died for us.
Much more then, being now justified by His blood,
we shall be saved from wrath through Him.*

Romans 5:8,9

(8.10.10.4.  All Hallows *or* Ellasgarth)

O Son of Man, O Son of God,
   Eternal grace Thy painful path had planned,
A heavy cross and agony of shame —
   The way ordained.

O death of Christ, O blood divine,
   O perfect life He lived, all for my gain,
Fulfilling all the law's demands, and more,
   He did attain.

O bitter cup, O costly task,
   To meet the wrath of God's own holiness!
The Saviour stood, and in my stead He died,
   My soul to bless.

O love of God, O wondrous grace,
   That such an angry death of anguish sore
Should pay my penalty and make me whole —
   O boundless store!

## God the Son

O wondrous flood of grace and love,
    Both mingled in the blood as He implored:
Can this be so, all this for me, my Lord?
    Thou art adored.

Peace through the blood of Christ alone,
    Peace with my God and peace within my soul,
Peace in that day when He will come at last,
    My all in all.

# 39

*For the wages of sin is death; but the gift of God is eternal life through Jesus Christ our Lord.*

Romans 6:23

(87.87.47.  Blaencefn)

Lord of all this vast creation,
    Rules supreme on all mankind,
Moved in time, displayed salvation,
    Incarnation, Son, so kind.
        Gift of heaven,
Hallelujahs ring the skies.

Man has fallen from his station
    Where he stood with God sublime;
Sin has marred the fair condition,
    Separated through man's crime.
        Cries for mercy
Came from hearts in dark despair.

Listen to the voice of judgement
    Ringing loud for all to hear,
Punishment the dreaded comment,
    These the wages that we bear;
        Lost without Him,
Hear our cry, O blessèd Lord!

## God the Son

Sovereign God, and God of mercy
Sent His Son to shed His blood,
Merit pure, and merit worthy
Satisfied His anger's flood;
Full atonement!
Justice smiles at all her own.

Gift of life, eternal value,
Granted to the sinners now,
With repentance, holy sorrow,
Faith from Christ Thou dost allow;
Chosen people,
Join the anthem of the elect.

# 40

*A new heart also will I give you, and a new Spirit will I put within you:*
*and I will take away the stony heart out of your flesh,*
*and I will give you a heart of flesh.*

Ezekiel 36:26

(C.M.  Salzburgh)

O living Lord of grace and truth,
We love Thy blessèd name;
For we have learned of Thine increase,
And of Thy wondrous fame.

For who has loved like God the Son,
And entered our estate?
Who for our good alone has won
A place, by God's dictate.

It must have been an act divine
To be so wondrous kind;
For in this rich and costly wine,
A pardon pure I find.

## God the Son

O, gaze upon the broken frame,
   And take the wine and bread;
For He has died with all our shame,
   To be our living Head.

For there is nought that I can bring
   To boast before His throne:
My fancied pride before this King
   Stands foolish and alone.

O turn mine eyes upon the cross,
   Remove this heart of stone;
That I may see what dreadful loss
   Thy mercy faced alone.

O lovely Lord, with precious blood,
   I cast my soul on Thee:
For I shall wash in Calvary's flood —
   Redeemed, my joyful plea.

# 41

*I beseech you therefore brethren, by the mercies of God,*
*that ye present your bodies a living sacrifice,*
*holy, acceptable unto God, which is your reasonable service.*

Romans 12:1

(88.88.88.  St. Chrysostom)

I saw an altar far away
With gentle Lamb that men did slay;
A costly place of bitter pain,
A cross the price that moved our stain.
The wrath of God faced Christ alone,
For sin of man He did atone.

## God the Son

O blessèd spot of joy and bliss,
A cleansing flow my heart did kiss;
A place where peace and mercy meet
In one embrace forever sweet.
Almighty God, blest Trinity,
For this my soul will worship Thee.

Then take my life for Thee alone,
And ever rule upon my throne,
As on the altar I recline,
A living sacrifice of Thine.
Lord, keep me with Thy lovely grace,
Transformed for all to see Thy face.

Fashions of earth now fade away,
Courses of evil must not stay:
Merciful Father, see Thy child,
Incline my heart with strength so mild.
Always secure in Thee I find
Sufficient grace and peace of mind.

Thy perfect will is my delight,
And in my heart renewing light:
Thus in my daily life I pray,
Delight in good, a holy way;
Wonderful change, that all may see
What God Almighty did for me.

# 42

*Behold, the half was not told me.*

1 Kings 10:7

(D.C.M. Rhos)

I heard about the Son of Man,
　His beauty failed to see;
And wandered far, and vainly ran,
　Believing I was free.
And then Thy kind restraining grace
　Upon my soul took hold.
I stood amazed, and saw Thy face —
　The half had not been told!

Thy mercy led me through the vale;
　My heart, with sorrow laid,
With trembling trust and visage pale,
　Beheld the price He paid.
Such majesty and dignity!
　Though piercing crown was worn;
This blood and sacrifice to me
　Brought peace and I was born.

O blessèd Jesus, lovely name,
　A rose amongst the thorns!
I cannot see why men defame,
　And this my heart now mourns.
O gracious Lord, hear now my praise,
　I on Thy bosom lean;
Immortal source, eternal grace,
　Thy beauty I have seen.

# 43

*And about the ninth hour Jesus cried with a loud voice,*
*saying, Eli, Eli, lama sabachthani? that is to say,*
*My God, My God, why hast Thou forsaken me?*

Matthew 27:46

(8.10.10.4.  Ellasgarth)

Incarnate God, of virgin born,
  Only begotten Son of God above:
Love of the Godhead now in human form,
  The King of love.

Angels proclaimed, promise of peace,
  Praising our God in glorious sweet accord:
Shepherds in fear, were told of man's release,
  In Christ the Lord.

Symbol of Kings, symbol of death,
  Symbol of Deity the wise men brought:
Gold, frankincense and myrrh, the gifts of earth;
  Yet Christ they sought.

God's will revealed, now men may tell
  Fulfilment true in Christ the word did bring;
Hour of the Cross and triumph over hell,
  For Christ is King.

# 44

*My sheep hear my voice, and I know them, and they follow me;*
*and I give unto them eternal life; and they shall never perish,*
*neither shall any man pluck them out of my hand.*

John 10:27,28

(76.76.D.  Bentley)

There is a Shepherd bidding,
　　Who calls His sheep by name;
His gentle voice compelling
　　To leave the paths of shame.
They hear Him in their wandering
　　From distant rock and range,
And long for His embracing;
　　Their way they cannot change.

Now see the blessèd Saviour,
　　Who seeks and finds His sheep;
His footsteps never falter,
　　He has the power to keep.
Behold the marks of suffering;
　　Where has the Shepherd been?
These wounds and blood, this mocking,
　　O, hast thou, sinner, seen?

O wanderer, see Him beckon,
　　His person drawing nigh;
Respond and call for pardon,
　　And He will hear thy cry.
For none can ever pluck thee
　　From those eternal hands;
The strength of God Almighty
　　Confirms the gracious bands.

God the Son

The plan which God unfolded
Was full of love and care.
The Saviour, who committed
Himself, His grace did share.
This Lord of peace we cherish,
Grants life that cannot fade;
And we shall never perish
In God's eternal shade.

# 45

*But He was wounded for our transgressions, He was bruised for our iniquities:*
*the chastisement of our peace was upon Him; and with His stripes we are healed.*
Isaiah 53:5

(88.88.D.  Trewen)

The Saviour's sad visage behold!
Despised and rejected of all;
His sorrow the prophets foretold,
With grief that was bitter as gall.
Our faces we turned, and our thought
Away from the Lamb of the cross;
Esteeming and shunning as nought
The One who has suffered such loss.

He carried our failure and sin,
On His blessèd shoulders, our shame;
The pain of our wandering for Him,
A burden, His heart did inflame.
O blessèd Redeemer of men!
Thy name is ineffably sweet;
We cling to Thy merits for heaven,
Adoring we fall at Thy feet.

## God the Son

The Saviour was wounded for me,
    Was bruised and chastised for my sake;
They led Him to Calvary's tree,
    And spat at the man at the stake.
The stripes of the Saviour, they heal,
    His blood for our sin does atone;
Amazing how grace will reveal
    The plan He accomplished alone!

A lamb to the slaughter, He came,
    From prison and judgement condemned.
They schemed for His end without shame,
    He never a word did defend.
Was ever a Saviour so meek,
    So mighty, and able to keep?
His grace to our hearts gently speaks
    And comforts the sinner that weeps.

My heart with Thy love Thou dost smite,
    Convincing my soul, so complete,
Thy Spirit revealing my plight,
    The shadow of hell at my feet.
O Saviour, have pity on me,
    Thy merits with mercy apply,
And endless my praises to Thee
    I'll sing as Thou callest me nigh.

# 46

*That Christ may dwell in your hearts by faith;*
*that ye, being rooted and grounded in love,*
*may be able to comprehend with all saints*
*what is the breadth, and length, and depth, and height;*
*and to know the love of Christ.*

Ephesians 3:17-19

(87.87.D. Prysgol)

Great and wondrous is the mystery
    Born in time thus Christ revealed.
Strange and glorious is the history:
    God incarnate, once concealed,
Lived and died and rose victorious
    Over sin and man's despair,
Shattered Satan's schemes disastrous,
    Granted grace and soul's repair.

Miracle beyond conception
    Of imagination's sphere,
This is God's own true salvation,
    Truth's reality draws near.
In our hearts there dwells a Saviour,
    There by faith, His gift of love
In our living, strengthened daily
    By the indwelling of the Dove.

Rich in Christ, and rich for ever,
    Rooted, grounded in His love;
O, the mercy of the Father!
    Giving wisdom from above;
Comprehension to the sinner,
    That our hearts may now be sealed
With the love of our Redeemer —
    O, the wonder now revealed!

Yet this love surpasses knowledge,
　　Knowing Him, and yet to know,
Living, learning every privilege,
　　Filled with God, whilst here below.
Far above all expectation,
　　He is able to fulfil
Strength within from this relation,
　　For it is the Father's will.

Praise His name for ages ever,
　　Let the heavens resound their joy;
For His mercies will not sever,
　　Nor His holiness destroy.
We have boldness now of access,
　　Paved by blood, the price of sin,
Confidence in Him, the sinless,
　　Faith of God now dwells within.

# 47

*For who hath known the mind of the Lord, that he may instruct him?*
*But we have the mind of Christ.*

1 Corinthians 2:16

(D.L.M.  Merthyr Tydfil)

All that the eye can ever see,
　　Or this poor mind can comprehend:
All, all are Thine, and nought can be
　　Outside Thy scope, each to Thee bend.
Beyond the regions of my sight,
　　And past the confines of my thought,
Is Thy vast, pure, compelling light,
　　Revealing all that Thou hast wrought.

## God the Son

Yet there are depths within Thy heart
    That throb with love and care for me,
And all my efforts to depart
    But bring me back Thy grace to see.
Compelling love, constraining grace
    That holds the great, and holds the small,
With firmer hold and sweet embrace,
    For none of Thine shall fail or fall.

Thou art the Father of my Lord,
    Who shed His blood to cover me
With righteousness, and dost afford
    A place of peace and purity.
His name is Jesus, Christ of God,
    I cling to Him, I love His name,
For He has borne the heavy rod
    A painful penalty and shame.

There is no path where I may tread,
    Nor any way from Thee to hide,
No solace, but the constant dread,
    If I do not with Thee abide.
Thy name is Jesus Christ my Lord,
    And all my life and soul is Thine, —
A conquest made by Thy blest sword,
    A victory won by grace divine.

# 48

*Let us run with patience the race that is set before us,*
*looking unto Jesus the author and finisher of our faith.*

Hebrews 12:1,2

(64.64.66.64.  The Path Divine)

Glory to Thee, my Lord,
  Infinite King;
Wonderful peace afford
  Under Thy wing!
Incarnate Deity,
Merciful Calvary,
This is my only plea:
  Hear my heart sing.

Glory I bring to Thee
  Not of mine own,
All Thou hast given me
  Now I return.
All Thine enabling grace
Leads me on life's long race,
Until I see Thy face,
  When I come home.

Glory belongs to Thee,
  To Thee alone;
Thieves we must never be
  Before Thy throne.
We are the lost now found,
Here on redemption ground,
Hearing the Gospel sound,
  No more to roam.

## God the Son

Glory and praises sweet
    Flow to Thee now;
True adoration meet
    See as we bow.
Glory to God above,
Father and Son of love
Spirit who, Holy Dove,
    Grace dost endow.

# 49

*And it shall come to pass, while my glory passeth by,*
*that I will put thee in a cleft of the rock,*
*and will cover thee with my hand while I pass by.*

Exodus 33:22

(76.76.D. Rutherford)

Thy grace, my God, is mighty,
    Sufficient for my need;
And from Thy wondrous bounty
    My soul will ever feed.
Thy matchless precious presence,
    So full of truth and grace,
Shall be my only preference:
    I'll ever seek Thy face.

Thy face, O my Redeemer,
    With countenance so fair,
Delights my heart with wonder:
    None can with Thee compare.
From wounds of merit costly
    Flow pardon, peace and joy,
O blessèd, blessèd Calv'ry!
    My God I will enjoy.

## God the Son

And yet, O Lord of mercy,
    Withhold Thy hand at times,
For when Thou dost embrace me
    My feeble frame declines.
The anguish of Thy glory
    My trembling soul can't bear:
I sink in human frailty,
    Without Thy covering care.

O fortify me, Saviour,
    With strength that comes from Thee;
Endue my soul, Redeemer,
    With sweet serenity.
I long to know such fulness,
    But grant me grace to stand,
A vessel with new firmness
    Controlled by Thy great hand.

# 50

*And to know the love of Christ, which passeth knowledge,*
*that ye might be filled with all the fulness of God.*

Ephesians 3:19

(C.M.  Penmachno)

There is a love that Christ alone
    Can give to hearts that seek:
A love that fills and keeps His own,
    And makes the mighty meek.

Such meekness, Lord, is strength divine,
    That leads to paths of grace:
That tells my heart that I am Thine,
    And shall behold Thy face.

## God the Son

The length and breadth no more can tell
  The depth and height of love:
It passes knowledge, like the swell
  Of gracious waves above.

There is a place where I may find
  The fulness of God's grace:
A path of faith and love, to bind
  God's promise and embrace.

O let me, Lord, pursue Thee now,
  The Christ of Calvary:
O stir my soul that I may bow,
  And plead my cause to Thee.

This promise, Thou wilt honour, Lord,
  To hearts that Thou hast moved:
O leave me not, but grace afford,
  And let Thy name be proved.

Exalt Thy name in hearts of stone,
  Now stirred to love Thy name:
For Thou art God, and Thou alone
  Canst spread Thy royal fame.

# 51

*For as in Adam all die, even so in Christ shall all be made alive.*
1 Corinthians 15:22

(8.10.10.4.  Ellasgarth)

In Eden fair, a place divine;
Image of God, stood man, created whole;
Through Satan's guile, he fell by sin's design:
  A guilty soul.

## God the Son

In ancient days, in Edom far,
There stood a warrior wounded there for me;
He trod the winepress bearing every scar
    Of love's decree.

In sad Gethsemane He prayed,
And drank the cup of pain, the Father's will;
For there He wept and angels Him sustained,
    As time stood still.

In God's full time, eternal plan,
My Saviour stood for me, and in my place,
He hung alone, the Son of God and Man;
    An act of grace.

In that great day, ordained above,
The Son of God will come unto His own;
The sons of grace and sons of sovereign love,
    To bring them home.

In that blest land, Jerusalem,
No tears are known, for God alone draws near.
The saints are glad and sing the great 'Amen',
    For God is here.

In songs of joy, I'll ever raise
My thankful heart, adoring God alone;
Forever satisfied, on Him I'll gaze
    Before His throne.

# 52

*Who being in the form of God, thought it not robbery to be equal with God:*
*but made Himself of no reputation, and took upon Him the form of a servant,*
*and was made in the likeness of men.*

Philippians 2:6,7

(C.M.  University)

Lord Jesus Christ, I worship Thee,
  Thou King of love and grace;
For Thou hast whispered I may see
  The glory of Thy face.

My Saviour gave Himself for me,
  With reputation, none!
O, such a death and agony
  Has my pure pardon won!

Nothing I give can Him repay,
  My Saviour and my joy;
Nothing I have can I display,
  Will ever grace employ.

Yet freely of Thy grace alone,
  I stand on ground secure;
Thou hast atoned and moved the stone
  To gates of life so sure.

O let me bring to Thee my love,
  The tithes of my own heart;
To give, and give, to Thee above,
  This holy, blessèd part.

How can these hands forget so soon
  Those pierced on a Cross?
How can this heart refuse a room
  And suffer such a loss?

## God the Son

O teach me Lord to understand
How Thou dost blessing give;
Fill Thou Thy storehouse by Thy hand,
And show me how to live!

# 53

*And, behold, the veil of the temple was rent in twain from the top*
*to the bottom; and the earth did quake, and the rocks rent.*

Matthew 27:51

(D.C.M.  St. Leonard's)

What piercing cry from cross of pain!
His lips the silence tore;
A finished work, our Lord was slain,
As all our sins He bore.
The veil is rent in temple sad,
All shadows now fulfilled;
An entry made to sanctuary glad,
As heaven and earth are stilled.

O rend the veil within my heart,
When darkness hides Thy face,
And bid my guilt and shame depart;
Thy mercy on me trace.
A ray of hope from Calvary
Lights up my soul with joy;
And all the hosts of darkness flee,
For none can me destroy.

O let me enter past the veil
Within these precincts pure,
And there delight in Thee, and hail
The glories that endure.
An open heart, an honest mind,
A life laid bare to see;
O keep me there for ever bind
My heart and soul to Thee.

# 54

*And when He had spoken these things, while they beheld,*
*He was taken up; and a cloud received Him out of their sight.*

Acts 1:9

(66.84.D. Leoni)

The Saviour now ascends
Before the Father's throne;
He pleads for us and now defends
Who are His own.
He gave us noble birth,
An act of grace in time,
He called us His, and prayed on earth,
'For they are Thine'.

Because He went on high,
On God's right hand to stand,
The Holy Spirit brings Him nigh
To every land.
Sweet messenger of grace,
Companion in our ways,
This wondrous name we'll not disgrace
In all our days.

A constant presence now,
Our Advocate and Friend;
Before our Saviour all will bow,
And to Him bend.
A comfort to each heart
With knowledge that He cares;
In life or death He'll not depart:
His kingdom shares.

# 55

*Lord, now lettest Thou Thy servant depart in peace, according to Thy word:*
*for mine eyes have seen Thy salvation.*

Luke 2:29,30

### (D.C.M. Forest Green)

All praise and honour to the child,
    In gentle arms who lay,
When Simeon took this undefiled,
    The Lord whom men did slay.
He gazed upon the little one,
    And gladness filled his breast;
His eyes beheld God's only Son,
    In whom all men are blest.

We rest in arms eternal, strong,
    Secure for evermore;
For we are found, to Him belong;
    Our souls He will restore.
The arms of grace encompass firm
    With pardon and with love;
Assurance does our hearts confirm,
    The gift of God above.

We gaze into the eyes of Him
    Who grants us peace of mind;
For we have seen the Saviour win
    Salvation for mankind.
We look to Jesus Christ our Lord,
    And rest in Him alone;
For we have hearkened to His word,
    The Lord who did atone.

The hope and light of all mankind,
    Emmanuel now displayed;
He fills our eyes and, men to find,
    Behold the price He paid!

God the Son

We worship Thee with heart and voice,
And praise Thy sweetest grace;
Recline our souls as we rejoice
To feel Thy blest embrace.


# 56

*Jesus Christ the same yesterday, and today, and forever.*
Hebrews 13:8

(88.88.D. Trewen)

A beautiful name I have heard,
With sound of salvation to me;
God's only begotten and Word,
This Jesus of blest Calvary.
Eternal, yet born into time,
Unchanging, for ever the same,
A Saviour in person sublime
Has taken our sin and our shame.

The burdens of life press me hard,
And weariness weighs like the hills;
Then Satan with wiles to retard
Surrounds my poor soul with all ills.
I then look to Jesus my Lord,
And find a new grace for the day;
New mercies fresh manna afford,
Which drive all my terrors away.

His person I'll never exhaust,
Unchanging yet ever anew:
Without Him I'm weak and I'm lost,
But with Him my strength does renew.
The mountains of hard unbelief
I'll move with the power of His name;
Although all I am is but brief,
My Saviour is ever the same.

## God the Son

Whenever I look on Thy face,
New beauties I'll ever behold:
I'll ever discover new grace,
The half cannot ever be told.
A Saviour so constant and true,
Immortal, eternal and pure;
Thy mercy is fresh as the dew
Reviving with grace to endure.

# 57

*Then went in also that other disciple, which came first to the sepulchre,*
*and he saw, and believed.*

John 20:8

(D.C.M. Petersham)

Dawn of the resurrection day
Has spread its glorious light,
And rolled the heavy stone away
Of unbelief's sad night.
O joy of heaven, this sweet concord
Of truth and mercy fair!
An empty grave, a living Lord
Thy gospel will declare.

O stand amongst us, Son of God,
And in our hearts grant grace
To be amidst the saints who trod
The path of faith's swift race.
We have not seen Thy wounds and scar,
We have not touched Thy side;
We have not followed Bethlehem's star;
Yet in Thee we abide.

### God the Son

Light of our hearts, hope of our souls
  Is Jesus Christ today;
For in one mighty act, He rolls
  The weight of sin away.
We thank Thee here that Thou didst come
  To die for our disgrace,
To rise again and so confirm
  The surety of Thy grace.

# 58

*But ye are come… to Jesus the mediator of the new covenant,*
*and to the blood of sprinkling*

Hebrews 12:24

(76.76.D.  Pen-yr-Yrfa)

We greet the Prince of Glory,
  The joy of heaven's delight.
We praise the Lord of Mercy
  Who dwells in perfect light.
He is the King of pardon,
  He is the King of grace;
He gave His life a ransom,
  We love His blessèd face.

From Sinai's fiery mountain
  The law called out for love;
The perfect satisfaction
  Of God in heaven above.
The Saviour, as a servant
  Fulfilled the law's demands,
He trod upon the serpent,
  Our sin was in His hands.

### God the Son

O blessèd hands of Jesus,
 The Lord of love and peace;
Thy wondrous love toward us
 Shall never, never cease.
Thy wounds of glad atonement
 In hands and feet and side,
Were wounds of rich redemption
 That ever will abide.

All hail to Thee Redeemer,
 The crowned King of kings!
Where thorns adorned a Saviour
 Made rich amongst all things.
We bow in glad surrender
 With sparkling souls made white;
Our life will ever render
 The songs of purest light.


# 59

*And if any man sin, we have an advocate with the Father,*
*Jesus Christ the righteous.*

1 John 2:1

(665.665.786. Jesu, Meine Freude)

Radiant in Thy glory,
I behold Thy mercy,
Blessèd Advocate.
Right hand of the Father,
There my rare Redeemer,
Lord compassionate!
Mercy's day at our last dawn,
Great Redemption, resurrection:
Glorious satisfaction.

## God the Son

See the Holy City,
Splendid in its beauty,
Royal realm supreme.
God has planned in wisdom,
At the consummation,
Days above a dream!
Death's dominion does not dare,
Tears and fears now gone for ever:
Welcome of our Father.

Heaven and home exalted,
Rest of all adopted,
Plan of love sublime.
Long were the afflictions,
Bitter persecutions,
In the scale of time.
Grace outweighs the fall and sin,
Hail incarnate, born of virgin,
Hail Almighty Sovereign!

# 60

*In whom we have redemption through His blood, even the forgiveness of sins.*
Colossians 1:14
(L.M. Glanllyfnwy)

Unmoved are they who in Thee stay
Rested and grounded in Thy way:
Upheld by grace Thy face to see,
The wonders of Thy Calvary.

Unchallenged are the ones who find
Sweet solace in such wounds so kind.
Unmeasured merit of the blood
The Saviour shed in gracious flood.

### God the Son

Unlimited the joys of those
Who find in Thee their calm repose:
Inheritance of joy and peace
From all afflictions sweet release.

Unnumbered blessings Thou dost give
To those who long and for Thee live:
Great are their hopes and great their joy
When Thy great grace does them employ.

Unmoved remain the saints of time,
Who stand secure in grace sublime:
No foe shall ever take away
The ones for whom our Lord did pray.


# 61

*I am the rose of Sharon, and the lily of the valleys.*
Song of Solomon 2:1
(C.M.  Southwell)

Belovèd of the Throne on High,
   The Everlasting Son,
Thou gavest Him to bring us nigh:
   Salvation for us won.

The Rose of Sharon is Thy name,
   So gentle and so fair:
Thy tender fragrance is the fame
   For every saint to share.

The lily of the valley fair
   Has found a resting place.
My heart a throne to One so meek
   Who tells of truth and grace.

## God the Son

Thine is the Morning Star so bright
That tells the heavens above,
The wonders of the Prince of Light,
His mercy and His love.

Jerusalem, awake to see
His majesty divine;
The King of Love, whose agony
Hath made Him ever mine.

Reluctant hearts O Lord forgive,
And bring us to our King;
Revive us now, that we may live,
Thy praises ever sing.


# 62

*I have finished the work which Thou gavest me to do*

John 17:4

(10 4.10 4.10 10.  Sandon)

Father forgive, they know not what they do,
To Me, Thy Son;
Father regard the penalty that's due
Which I have won.
Now is fulfilled the plan of heaven above
To bring the sons of earth into Thy love.

Thou dost remember the poor sinner's plight
On Calvary;
Thou dost recall us by Thy Word of might
To bow the knee.
Great is the promise of Thy paradise
Today is ours the gen'rous beauteous prize.

# God the Son

Thou didst regard the women at the cross,
      And Mary's heart.
Thou didst enable them to bear the loss,
      And not depart.
Comfort Thou gavest Mary in her woe
And won the vict'ry over every foe.

Loud was the cry upon that lonely hill;
      My God, My God.
Painful the pardon for a world of ill:
      O cruel rod.
Forsaken, stricken, chosen beyond time,
The Son of God with mercy so sublime.

O blessèd Saviour longing there for me:
      His holy thirst.
O sacred head that bowed in agony,
      Yet placed Thee first.
Glory to God now fills the sinner's soul
With peace and pardon from his heavy toll.

Finished the work of God's eternal plan:
      Now satisfied.
Behold the triumph of the rainbow's span:
      The Crucified.
Angels adore and heaven resounds the praise;
Its Halleljuah's whole creation raise.

Into Thy hands O God of glory now
      My spirit give;
Unto the Lord of all creation bow,
      Who does forgive.
There is a path ordained and now prepared
For souls who seek and find a God who cared.

## God the Son

Righteous the Son who paid the penalty
  In that strange hour;
Sinless the Son who went to Calvary;
  And yet in power
Sins are forgiven and an entrance made
To heaven and glory which shall never fade.


# 63

*Who is this that cometh from Edom, with dyed garments from Bozrah?*
  *this that is glorious in his apparel, travelling in the greatness*
  *of his strength? I that speak in righteousness, mighty to save.*

Isaiah 63:1

(64.64.66.64.  Builth)

Who is this fearful foe
  With presence chill —
His gaze and word of woe,
  Unbending will?
He comes to high and low,
With unrelenting flow;
The fear of all below,
  This Death so still.

Yet men forget their end,
  From God they flee:
They on themselves depend,
  With pride their plea.
Yet all their life is vain,
And foolish all their claim;
And though they death disdain,
  They are not free.

### God the Son

Who is this Warrior true
Who now appears?
A mighty form who slew
Our dreadful fears!
Begotten from above,
With grace of heaven's Dove,
He is the Lord of love:
Their debt He clears.

Now sin and death have failed
In all their scheme;
And Satan's work destroyed:
God's strength is seen.
The price of sin is paid,
A path of heaven is laid,
With life that cannot fade:
O glorious theme!

# 64

*Forasmuch as ye are manifestly declared to be the epistle of Christ ministered by
us, written not with ink, but with the Spirit of the living God;
not in tables of stone, but in fleshy tables of the heart.*

2 Corinthians 3:3

(87.87.D.  Arfon *or* Corinth)

O, have mercy, gracious Saviour,
Look upon this heart of sin,
Which has nothing more to offer
But the stubborn pride within.
On the wall the dreadful writing,
Words of judgement and despair;
In the balances found wanting,
Jesus, Saviour, hear my prayer.

## God the Son

O, give light and understanding,
  Spirit of the living God;
In Thy grace Thy truth revealing,
  Open Thou Thy precious Word.
Tell of virtues, grace and kindness
  That from Calvary's hill do spring;
Speak of mercy and forgiveness
  That my soul may ever sing.

Dip the pen, O Lord of glory,
  In the blood of Jesus shed;
Write upon our hearts the story
  Of atonement fully made.
Once inscribed upon the tablet
  Of our hearts let none erase;
There unmoved let it be fixèd,
  Read for all eternal days.

*trans. Edmund Owen*


# 65

Based on Song of Solomon.

(D.C.M.  Rhos)

The Lord drew near my love to find,
  And called me to His side.
With sad reluctance I declined,
  And turned away to hide.
My lonely soul in sudden fear,
  Cried out His lovely Name:
But He was gone, I knew not where,
  And left me in my shame.

## God the Son

What have I done, this soul of mine,
　To grieve the dearest One?
To drive Him from my breast, yet pine
　Not to be left alone.
Shunned by my friends, and all did spurn,
　In bitter tears I mourn;
Return, O Holy One, return,
　My soul shall no more roam.

O daughters of Jerusalem,
　Beloved is His Name:
Turn not away, do not condemn
　And leave me in my shame.
O let me of my longing share
　For Jesus Christ my Lord.
He is the One, my soul does care
　To stay in sweet accord.

He is the Rose of Sharon rare,
　The Lily of the Vale,
His countenance so fine, most fair,
　His strength can never fail.
He is the lover of my heart,
　My yearning soul desires:
My ravished heart will not depart:
　My eager soul inspires.

I hear a sound, a gentle sound,
　Yet strong in powerful grace:
At last my soul by Him is found,
　I shall behold His face.
He is the Bright and Morning Star,
　This Christ of Calvary.
O'er hill and vale and mountains far
　He calls, He comes for me.

# 66

Based on Isaiah 40.

(D.C.M.  Ellacombe)

O comfort of my longing heart
　Look down from heaven on me.
Reveal to me I have a part
　In Thine eternity.
Yet how shall I, the dust of earth,
　To glorious heaven attain
Unless Thy mercy gives me birth?
　For this my Lord was slain.

O Thou who dwellest in the heights,
　Thy sovereign rule to fear
When all creation in Thy sight
　As dust and sand appear.
Yet in Thy mercy and Thy grace
　This dust may worship Thee;
We rise on high to see Thy face
　Through costly Calvary.

Have we not known, have we not heard
　Thy miracles of old?
Thy people who have loved Thy word
　Such wondrous tales have told.
O look in pity yet once more
　Upon Thy heritage,
And cause Thy people to adore
　The God of every age.

We rise like eagles in full flight
　When Thou art by our side.
We run, we walk with hearts so light,
　Within Thy love abide.

## God the Son

For they who wait upon the Lord
    Shall never be dismayed;
The word of God, Thy mighty sword,
    In splendour now displayed.

# 67

*Behold, I have graven thee upon the palms of my hands.*

Isaiah 49:16

(C.M. Saron)

Show me Thy hands, a myriad names
    Are written in Thy palm,
Of sinners saved from Satan's flames,
    Now praise with hymn and psalm.

What wondrous grace, what strange design
    Of love within Thy heart,
Caused sinful man to sin resign
    And find in Thee a part.

What rich inheritance divine
    Without corruption's lies:
Here nought defiles this home of Thine
    And no one ever dies.

O show me, Lord, and calm my fear;
    My name is written there
On Thy pure hand with imprint clear,
    That I am in Thy care.

My sinful life I now confess
    With guilt my hands hang low:
O look upon my deep distress,
    And mercy, mercy show.

## God the Son

'Tis then I see those hands so fair,
   They beckon now to me:
My name in blood is written there,
   At costly Calvary.

Engraved for ever in Thy heart
   My faith lays hold on thee.
No, never more from Thee depart,
   Or move from Calvary.

For now I see the mystery
   Unfolding to new eyes:
The God eternal — Trinity
   On whom the world relies.

For far beyond the birth of time
   My name was written there.
Eternal grace, with joy sublime
   Thy matchless Name declare.

Rejoice, rejoice O happy soul;
   Immortal is thy state.
The grace that sought and made thee whole
   In newness did create.

# 68

*Father, the hour is come; glorify Thy Son, that Thy Son also may glorify Thee:
As Thou hast given Him power over all flesh, that He should give
eternal life to as many as Thou hast given Him.*

John 17:1-2

(C.M. Bangor)

The hour is come, the Saviour cried,
    To glorify Thy name:
For us He lived, for us He died,
    To take away our shame.

The Father to the Son now gave
    His own to glorify;
His very own, that Christ might save
    This lovely legacy.

We hide within the Saviour's prayer,
    The shadow of His grace;
The sunshine of His costly care,
    For evermore embrace.

When all seemed lost and we alone
    At desolation stared;
This we believed, we were His own:
    He prayed because He cared.

Yes, we believe that we are Thine,
    The gifts of God to Thee,
And Thou art ours, our Friend Divine
    To love eternally.

Eternal life Thou dost bestow
    To know Thee, and adore;
For heaven to us, is Thee to know,
    And dwell for evermore.

# GOD THE HOLY SPIRIT

# 69

*But ye shall receive power, after that the Holy Ghost is come upon you:
and ye shall be witnesses unto me.*

Acts 1:8

(88.88.88.  St. Catherine)

Blest Holy Spirit, Breath Divine,
We thank Thee for Thy work sublime
In bringing sinners to the place,
To see the riches of God's grace;
The cleansing blood, amazing flow,
When Jesus Christ died here below.

Thy work reveals and shows our need,
Opens our eyes to sin's foul deed;
Swiftly repairs us to God's side,
And, finding there, we can abide,
With full forgiveness, blessèd peace —
Glory to God and grace increase.

Thou art the One who sanctifies,
Pointing which path before us lies
Ordained of God, that we should walk,
Enabled by Thy wondrous work —
A path devoid of sin and lust,
A path of holiness and trust.

O Paraclete, Thy blessèd gift
Enabled men, with power so swift,
To preach the Word of God with sign,
And for this now our hearts repine.
Hear us, we plead, with unction sweet
Baptize Thy saints, Thy promise meet.

'Revive Thy work' is all our cry,
Grant Pentecostal waves of joy:
A wondrous sight when men believe,
Constrained of God for sin to grieve.
Spirit Divine, with wind and flame,
Thine influence spread, in Jesus' Name.

# 70

*Woe is me! for I am undone; because I am a man of unclean lips,
and I dwell in the midst of a people of unclean lips:
for mine eyes have seen the King, the Lord of hosts.*

Isaiah 6:5

(64.64.66.64.  Glanhafren *or* Builth)

Create in us, O Lord,
  A holy fire;
Thy word a flaming sword
  Our hearts inspire.
Thy glories to declare,
Thy grace beyond compare,
Thy love with Thee to share,
  We now aspire.

Descend, O Holy Dove,
  With words of peace,
With blaze of truth and love
  On earth increase.
O stir our souls today
To seek Thy wondrous way;
For Thou hast come to stay:
  Then grace release.

God the Holy Spirit

Repeat Thy word of joy
    To us on earth,
And make Thy church employ
    Its saving worth.
O grant a refuge sweet,
A place for us to meet,
Thy holy presence greet:
    To hope give birth.

# 71

*And because ye are sons, God has sent forth the Spirit of His Son
into your hearts, crying, Abba, Father.*

Galatians 4:6

(C.M. Dublin)

Outstretch Thy wings, O holy Dove,
    And show Thy generous span
Of love and mercy from above,
    To heal the wounds of man.

The wounds of sin, without, within,
    From Fall and Satan's wile,
Bring separation, fruit of sin,
    And hide my Saviour's smile.

The cry of God now rends the air,
    'Where art thou, child of Mine?'
In nakedness and soul's despair
    Man hid — O, sad decline!

The Serpent's sting both hard and sore
    Had wounded all mankind:
Then came the Saviour to restore,
    With cords of love to bind.

## God the Holy Spirit

O blessèd flight of pure delight
   Is Thine, blest Spirit pure,
For Thou dost bring my soul a sight
   Of grace that will endure.

I see the blood my Saviour shed
   For sin's hard penalty;
I'll not forget how mercy sped,
   And set my spirit free.

Faith and repentance, gifts of grace,
   Are granted to my heart;
As I now long for Thine embrace,
   Such love Thou dost impart.

For now I find my soul with joy
   In folds of mercy sweet;
For there is no one can destroy
   Communion at God's feet.

# 72

*And suddenly there came a sound from heaven as a rushing mighty wind, and it*
*filled the house where they were sitting.*
*And there appeared unto them cloven tongues like as of fire,*
*and it sat upon each of them.*

Acts 2:2,3

(66.84.D.  Leoni)

The Holy Ghost has come
And shed His strength abroad;
The waiting Church, no longer dumb,
Extols her Lord.
Upon them all He came
Together as they prayed,
A mighty sight of wind and flame,
God's power displayed.

The promise of the Lord
Is now fulfilled in time;
The truth of Christ, a shining sword,
Is all sublime.
The gospel now applied
Brings hope and glorious light,
And happiness to those who sighed:
In Christ delight.

O gentle Dove of grace,
Who causes men to search,
Work on in hearts which in disgrace
Thy law besmirch.
For Thou alone canst bring
The lost to Jesu's feet,
Present the rebel to the King
For pardon sweet.

God the Holy Spirit

O Father, hear our cry,
In Jesu's name we ask;
The Spirit give, do not deny,
For Thy great task.
Behold a fallen race,
A church in weary state;
Baptise Thy children, grant this grace:
The hour is late.

# 73

*And hope maketh not ashamed; because the love of God is shed abroad in our*
*hearts by the Holy Ghost which is given us.*

Romans 5:5

(87.87.47.  Dismissal)

Show my soul this blessèd Saviour,
Visit me, O Holy Dove;
Let me see and let me ponder
On the merit of His love.
Grace and mercy
Flow from Him for fallen man.

Touch my heart with Thy redemption;
Quicken me, Lord, with Thy grace;
Grant me cleansing, and an unction,
With a vision of Thy face.
Smile upon me;
Let this pardon me embrace.

### God the Holy Spirit

Draw my heart in deep affection
  To my Saviour and my Lord,
With desire of Thy direction,
  Dwelling on Thy Holy Word.
    Give me wisdom;
  Guide my steps, and rule my life.

Turn my gaze in time of sorrow,
  There by faith to rest on Thee;
Teach me how to see the morrow
  Lightened by eternity.
    Giving honour,
  For all things Thou doest well.

Victor now, O fair condition,
  In the conquest of Thy might;
Who can shake this sure foundation
  As I stand in glorious light?
    I will praise Thee
  With a song of victory.

# 74

*Therefore if any man be in Christ, he is a new creature:*
*old things are passed away; behold, all things are become new.*
2 Corinthians 5:17

(C.M. Crimond)

What is this stirring in my breast
  That draws me, Lord, to Thee,
To seek the things I did detest,
  And long Thy face to see?

## God the Holy Spirit

It must have been Thy hand alone
That caused my heart to mourn,
And showed me One who did atone
And all my sins has borne.

Amazing is Thy gentle way:
Although inflicting pain,
It is Thy hand that does allay,
To take away my stain.

O Holy Ghost, this is Thy sphere,
To help my soul abide,
Rich wounds to show and thrust of spear
In His dear, blessèd side.

My heart is full: I thank Thee now
For all that Thou hast done;
With mercy rich, Thou didst endow;
My soul with grace has won.

O satisfy, my soul delight,
In holy pastures pure,
To learn of Thee, to walk aright,
And to the end endure.

Thy holy unction to the meek,
Bestowed at Pentecost,
I long to know, that I may speak
To win for Thee the lost.

# 75

*And suddenly there came a sound from heaven as of a rushing mighty wind.*

Acts 2:2

(L.M. Duke Street)

There is a path from heaven above
    Through hills and vales beyond our sight,
Where gentle breezes of Thy love
    Caress our hearts with glorious light.

Thy light alone can scatter far
    And cause this dimness to depart,
These heavy clouds which always mar
    And hide the smile of Thy pure heart.

O Breath of Heaven, eternal Spring,
    Thou pure, celestial Dove of grace,
O wing Thy truth, and let us sing
    The praises of the Prince of peace.

When will the sky with radiance shine,
    With favoured smile of heaven's grace?
O lift the gloom with wind divine,
    And warm our hearts with Thine embrace.

# 76

Based on Romans 8.

(D.C.M.  Kingsfold)

O send Thy Spirit to Thy child
   And whisper, 'Thou art mine';
O tell my soul in accents mild
   Of surety divine.
My heart shall leap, with rapid pace;
   To Thee my soul shall fly;
Reclining there, to seek Thy face,
   And 'Abba Father,' cry.

It is Thy Spirit who declares
   Adoption to my heart;
A child of grace, who glory shares:
   No, never more to part.
This deep assurance Thou dost give
   That moves my heart with joy;
The love of God in me to live,
   This, no one can destroy.

The witness of Thy Spirit shows
   That I am surely Thine;
The sweet embrace when mercy flows
   From heart and source divine.
Joint heirs with Christ, strange mystery
   Of mystic union rare;
Thy chosen children look to Thee,
   Thy matchless grace declare.

If God be for us who can dare
   Dismay, or spoil this bliss?
There is no love that can compare
   With such a love as His.

This love, now shed, so rich and free,
    Enfolds me in His grace;
In this I boast, His love to me,
    To live and see His face.


# 77

*And you hath he quickened, who were dead in trespasses and sins.*
                                                        Ephesians 2:1
(D.C.M.  Vox Dilecti)

I thank Thee for that silent touch
    In secret changed my heart;
Removed the cause of heaven's reproach,
    Bade sin's domain depart.
O breath of hope and holiness,
    Sweet messenger of light;
O Holy One my heart did bless
    And grant my soul new sight.

What deep distress weighed down my soul,
    Like mountains of despair;
My soul cried out to be made whole,
    My ruins to repair!
He turned my eyes from sin and shame
    To see His glorious face;
His gaze of mercy like a flame
    Revived my soul with grace.

O Son of God, the crucified,
    The choice of heaven above,
Descended to our depths and died,
    In that great act of love.
What gratitude can ever tell
    Of such a debt to pay;
That death of death that conquered hell
    And saved us for that Day?

## God the Holy Spirit

My soul will never turn away,
  The old ways to desire;
What wondrous waves of grace now sway
  My will, His way aspire.
For God Himself, my end, my aim,
  My everlasting store;
Anew in Christ, I will attain
  His heaven, and Him adore.


# 78

*And you hath he quickened, who were dead in trespasses and sins.*

Ephesians 2:1

(L.M.  Antwerp)

O blessèd day, O wondrous dawn,
  When Thou O Holy Spirit came
And touched my heart, and I was born
  To life with God, to end my shame.

No more to roam the realms of sin,
  Blind to my state and Satan's hold;
Called by my God to live with Him,
  And leave the depths of death untold.

By grace I rise and turn to Thee,
  And leave the idols of desire;
Through faith I come to Calvary
  And see my Saviour there expire.

O tender love, extended there
  Upon a cross, for sin He paid.
O wondrous wounds to One so fair:
  For all my sin on Him was laid.

## God the Holy Spirit

I lift my gaze to His dear face,
    And stand forgiven in His sight;
He took away my sad disgrace
    And looked upon me with delight.

O blessèd Jesus, grace does share;
    As God, as man, His love He shows;
Robed in His beauty, now I wear
    The righteousness He thus bestows.

Safe, safe am I in arms of grace,—
    A place prepared by love divine;
One day to see His lovely face
    And hear Him tell me 'thou art Mine'.

# THE GOSPEL

## 79

*Whom shall I send, and who will go for us? Then said I, Here am I; send me.*

Isaiah 6:8

(87.87.D.  Dim Ond Iesu *or* Lux Eoi)

Have you heard the voice of Jesus
    Softly pleading with your heart?
Have you felt His presence glorious,
    As He calls your soul apart,
With a love so true and loyal,
    Love divine that ever flows
From a Saviour, righteous, royal,
    And a cross that mercy shows?

Have you heard the voice of mercy
    Granting peace and pardon pure?
Have you felt the balm of Calvary
    Binding all your wounds secure?
Was there ever such salvation?
    Was there ever care like this?
See the Saviour's grief and passion,
    Grace and mercy's gentle kiss.

Have you heard the Saviour calling
    All to leave and follow Him?
Have you felt His Person drawing
    With compulsion lives to win?
Hearken to His invitation,
    To the music of God's grace;
Let the peace of God's salvation
    Fill your soul, and love embrace.

## The Gospel

Will you hear the voice of Jesus
    Calling home to mansions fair?
Will you know the promise precious,
    And the Shepherd's tender care?
Yes, if you in life responded
    To God's grace and gospel sound:
For they never are confounded
    Who believed and Jesus found.


# 80

*Thou art my hiding place; Thou shalt preserve me from trouble;*
*Thou shalt compass me about with songs of deliverance.*

Psalm 32:7

(88.6.D. Buddugoliaeth)


O Lord what work of grace is this,
That brought my soul from grief to bliss.
    O blessèd, wondrous name!
It is the Lord, whose mighty hands
Outstretched to meet the law's demands,
    And brought me from my shame.

My silent tongue but hid my pain,
My stricken conscience roared in vain;
    My moisture turned to drought.
Then mercy came and caused my soul
To come to Thee to make it whole,
    Dispelling all my doubt.

In gentle ways, Thy tender grace
Now led my soul to seek Thy face;
    Thy glory to behold.
My hiding place is found in Thee,
Thy merit is my only plea;
    And this shall make me bold.

## The Gospel

For there are times when Thou art found,
When floods of sorrows surge around
To drive me to despair.
The name of Christ, I will confess,
And in this hiding place will rest;
Secure in Jesus' care.

# 81

*Where art thou?*

Genesis 3:9

(76.76.D.  Kilmorey *or* Ewing)

The voice of God eternal
Was heard in Eden far,
'Mid silence that was fearful,
For sin had come to mar.
Where art thou, child created,
Where hidest thou from Me?
For sin has man defeated,
God's face he could not see.

A separation woeful
From God and hope and life,
Despair and death so painful,
A way of grief and strife.
The serpent so beguiling
Enticed mankind to fall,
The whole creation writhing,
From Satan's tempting call.

The Saviour to the victory
From heaven to earth came down;
He came to show God's mercy
And move the Father's frown.

## The Gospel

Upon His blessèd shoulders
  Our Saviour took our shame,
And paid the price for sinners;
  Who can forget His name?

Where art thou, O poor sinner,
  In death and sin's dark night?
O listen to the wonder
  Of words of truth and light.
O turn thy gaze to Calvary
  Where Jesus calls thee back;
From hiding come for mercy,
  In Christ thou wilt not lack.

O wondrous restoration,
  An act of grace sublime!
The news of man's salvation
  Was planned by love divine.
What peace and joy is given
  To those who hear His voice
To come and be forgiven,
  And in His grace rejoice.

# 82

*And when they were come to the place,*
*which is called Calvary, there they crucified Him.*

Luke 23:33

(D.C.M. Rhos)

What is this scene upon a hill,
   In heat of sun and sound,
Of hatred poised to strike and kill
   The Saviour, sore and bound?
O rarest place of penalty,
   Golgotha's death of death,
Where sin and death were made to flee,
   We greet this living breath.

What is this cross of heavy wood
   With sorrow sad weighed down,
Where Jesus Christ bore suffering rude
   With thorns of pain as crown?
O drop of mercy spilled for us,
   Which spoke of love and truth;
A mission that removed the curse
   And fear of death uncouth.

What is this view I now behold,
   My heart and soul amazed?
His bettered form, by Judas sold;
   I on His beauty gazed.
Beyond the cross, a cave, the sky,
   A risen Saviour fair;
With saving hope and glorious cry
   Salvation to declare.

# 83

*Because strait is the gate, and narrow is the way,*
*which leadeth unto life, and few there be that find it.*

Matthew 7:14

(D.C.M.  Kingsfold)

I heard about a narrow way
    That leads to mansions fair,
A way of danger night and day,
    Where Satan waits to tear.
The pilgrim on this living path
    Must steadfast keep his pace,
And look to Jesus Christ, who hath
    Sufficient strength and grace.

There is a way both broad and sweet
    To draw the human gaze;
We in our frailty rush to greet
    Each sin and foolish craze:
Yet, if I look beyond, I see
    An end of bitter pain,
Where Satan holds, and none can flee,
    And I shall call in vain.

O spare me Lord, from such an end,
    And grant me grace to see
That I must call, and I must bend,
    And come to Calvary.
O let me find within my breast
    A holy sorrow's tear,
And cry to Thee in my distress
    To find that Thou art near.

### The Gospel

Thou art the way my soul did hear
That leads me to that home;
I find in Thee a friend so dear,
No longer need I roam.
Thou art my Saviour, Lord and King,
And glorious Advocate;
And this I know, that Thou wilt bring
Thine own through heaven's gate.

# 84

*And the eyes of them that see shall not be dim,*
*and the ears of them that hear shall hearken.*

Isaiah 32:3

(87.87.D. Dusseldorf)

God of righteousness and mercy,
Grant Thy grace to those who cry
For a knowledge of Thy glory,
And Thy wondrous love on high.
Touch our eyes with healing vision;
From our minds this dimness move.
Let us see Thy great salvation;
Reach our hearts, as grace we prove.

Blessèd are the eyes that see Thee
As their Saviour and their King,
Ears that hear the Prince of Calvary
Speaking words that comfort bring.
In the wilderness a shadow
From the scorching of the fray;
Now a tenderness in sorrow:
By this Rock we'll ever stay.

In the tempest and the fury
    Of the anger of all ill,
Satan's host in cruel hurry
    Crowds our souls with accents shrill.
In our conflict, this our haven,
    Rock eternal, love's embrace;
Thou wilt ever spread confusion,
    Scatter foes and grant us grace.

This assurance comforts ever
    All Thy children in life's way,
For Thy promises have never
    Failed the weakest in that day.
Thou hast granted this outpouring
    Of Thy Spirit and Thy love,
Peace and quietness now giving
    As we gaze on Him above.

# 85

*Who his own self bare our sins in his own body on the tree.*

1 Peter 2:24

(87.87.  Cross of Jesus)

Rich the wood that bore the Saviour;
    Sad the nails that held Him there.
Yet they knew not of the horror
    Of the hate that men did dare.

Wise the prophets in the pages
    Of past centuries of time;
Joined with joy the laden sages,
    In their gifts to Christ sublime.

## The Gospel

Strange the sight, to men of sorrow,
    Was the cross, a place of death;
Such the eternal Son did borrow
    There to breathe His latest breath.

Yet the breath of life eternal
    Was the gift He gave to men,
Saving them from hell infernal:
    Let the people say 'Amen!'

# 86

*Let not your hearts be troubled: ye believe in God, believe also in me.*

John 14:1

(66.84.D. Dolwyddelan)

The mansions of the Lord
Are fair beyond compare;
The house of God will peace afford:
    To all declare.
See Jesus Christ has died
For those who once did roam;
And He alone can be our guide
    To bring us home.

Let not your troubled heart
Dismay in doubt and die;
Believe in God, do not depart;
    Now hear His cry.
The way to God above
Is only through His Son;
No other path, but by His love
    So dearly won.

## The Gospel

Look to the Saviour now,
Embrace His glorious form;
The way, truth, life He will endow
In gospel warm.
Complete in all He is,
Conforming to God's will;
A destined death by traitor's kiss
He did fulfil.

To all who trust in Him
God's word will never fall;
For He will guide and gather in
His children all.
The gentle Christ behold,
Who shed His blood so free;
Comes for His own, leads to the fold
His family.

The peace of God is strong,
And far above this earth;
It is the gift and happy song
Of heaven's worth.
This peace of heart and mind
That stays in storm and care,
Which God bestows to those who find
This Saviour fair.

# THE CHURCH OF CHRIST

# 87

*Behold how good and how pleasant it is for brethren to dwell together in unity!*

Psalm 133:1

(C.M.  Lloyd)

Behold, how blessèd is the place
　　Where brethren meet in love;
For they have known the Spirit's grace,
　　As gentle as a dove.

Precious the brow that feels the balm
　　Of healing incense sweet;
The savour of eternal calm
　　Its glorious God now greet.

Silent the dew on Zion's hills,
　　Eternal stillness lies;
The promise of a God who wills
　　His bountiful supplies.

Command the blessing there, O Lord
　　Of everlasting life;
Compel Thy people by Thy word
　　To cease from sinful strife.

Come quickly to Thy people, now,
　　And hear our humble cry;
Grant us Thy blessing as we bow
　　In contrite unity.

## The Church of Christ

Sweet is the balm and fresh the dew
   Of Thy redeeming grace;
Thy presence, real to us, yet few;
   We see Thy beauteous face.

Now let Thy blessing leap abroad
   Reviving sons of light;
Many shall praise their new-found Lord,
   The God of their delight.


# 88

*For we know that if our earthly house of this tabernacle were dissolved,*
*we have a building of God, a house not made with hands,*
*eternal in the heavens.*

2 Corinthians 5:1

(88.88.88.  St. Catherine)

Awake, my soul, the view behold,
Gaze on this splendour yet untold;
A glorious sight, a holy throne,
And God regarding all His own:
For He is Lord and God divine,
Whose grace and glory ever shine.


This earthly life and vanity,
Like mist and vapour, fade and flee;
Search as we may to be secure,
All pass away and we are poor.
This house of time is quickly spent,
Our mortal frame, a shifting tent.

### The Church of Christ

A house we have, not made by hand,
A tabernacle that will stand;
The plan of God, with mercy fair,
Constructed by His loving care;
A dwelling place, sweet work of grace,
Where we shall see the Master's face.

We know the terror of the Law,
And tremble at the sight with awe:
Yet we have known, and we have seen
A wondrous truth where we can lean.
A shaft of mercy love unfolds,
A robe of righteousness enfolds.

For in this royal home above,
We shall be clothed in gown of love;
Our nakedness gone clean away,
True righteousness is our display.
The blood of Christ will justice meet,
The judgement throne, a mercy seat.


# 89

*The battle is not yours, but God's.*

2 Chronicles 20:15

(87.87.337. Bryn Calfaria *or* Groeswen)

Who is this we see approaching
        With a multitude arrayed?
Satan's host is now encroaching
        On the Church for which Christ paid.
                Hear our cry,
                Grace apply,
Come and tell us Thou art nigh!

## The Church of Christ

Pressing is the host of darkness,
Bringing horror in its sway,
Causing us to doubt Thy kindness,
And to fall in deep dismay.
Take our fear,
Every tear,
Show our hearts that Thou art near.

Hear the Word of comfort glorious,
As it fills the sky above,
Telling us the power tremendous
Of our ancient God of love.
Do not fight!
I will plight
All my strength before Thy sight.

God of Israel, our defender—
He is Lord and God of all;
He commands us to remember
Gospel truth and bitter gall.
Jesus died,
And applied
Precious merit when we cried.

Now our eyes are on the Saviour
Who is Captain of our band;
His the battle, His the favour,
His the victory by His hand.
Sing His praise,
Ever raise
Glorious sound when trumpets blaze!

# 90

*But ye come unto Mount Sion, and unto the city of the living God,*
*the heavenly Jerusalem, and to an innumerable company of angels,*
*to the general assembly of the church of the firstborn.*

Hebrews 12:22,23

(87.87.D. Prysgol *or* Blaenwern)

Shake the earth, O mighty Saviour!
　　Let Thy voice like trumpet sound,
Full of strength and purest grandeur,
　　Stirring all the lost now found.
Sinners trembling, saints rejoicing,
　　As He calls His heavenly throng;
Hear new voices now proclaiming
　　Hallelujah gospel song!

We are come to this assembly
　　Of our Judge and of the Lamb,
Triune splendour dressed in mercy;
　　None of His shall come to harm.
See the firstfruits, Christ-begotten;
　　Read their names upon His palm;
They shall never be forgotten—
　　This shall be their happy psalm.

See the Saviour's exultation,
　　Son of God and Son of Man!
Now we see the consummation
　　And fulfilment of His plan.
Listen to the acclamation,
　　Ringing loud the heavens to hear,
Thanking God for our salvation
　　And for Jesus Christ so dear.

# 91

*What are these which are arrayed in white robes? and whence came they?*

Revelation 7:13

(86.886. Rest)

Around the throne of God above
　　There stands a glorious throng;
They tune their harps to themes of love,
Enabled by the Holy Dove
　　To sing the gospel song.

The music of the heavenly choir
　　Delights the hearts of all;
With chords of grace, on harp and lyre,
They tell of Satan's end of fire
　　In lake of bitter gall.

But who are these arrayed in white
　　And gowns of purity?
They are the saints who bathed in light
Do now appear, a glorious sight,
　　From sin and death set free.

This act of mercy we behold
　　Was planned by wondrous Three:
The Father's choice; a Saviour sold
For sin and death, an act so bold;
　　The Spirit leads to Thee.

The Church of Christ

# 92

*And I heard a great voice out of heaven saying, Behold, the tabernacle of God is
with men, and He will dwell with, them, and they shall be His people, and God
Himself shall be with them, and be their God.*

Revelation 21:3

(C.M.  St. Bernard)

Jerusalem will come to earth
 Adorned in sweet array,
And all things new, celestial worth,
 Proclaims the gracious day.

The tent of God, the voice did tell,
 Is pitched for every saint,
That they forevermore may dwell
 In Him without restraint.

The Lord, with tender, gracious hand,
 Shall wipe all tears away,
And gently show the purpose grand
 Of His own perfect way.

For death's sharp sting He will destroy,
 With glorious, vital life;
The blood of Christ brings peace and joy,
 And conquest in the strife.

To dwell with God is better far,
 And blessedness shall stay;
For sorrow, tears shall never mar,
 And pain shall pass away.

We'll rest in Jesus Christ our Head,
 His name is Lover, Friend;
Our thirsty souls He'll gently lead
 To waters without end.

# 93

*O that Thou wouldest rend the heavens, that Thou wouldest come down,*
*that the mountains might flow down at Thy presence.*

Isaiah 64:1

(87.87.D. Prysgol)

Rend the heavens Thou Prince of Glory,
  Melt the mountains with Thy grace;
Pour Thy presence, show Thy mercy
  And the radiance of Thy face.
We believe that Thou art able
  In Thy greatness and Thy love;
Make the nations fear and tremble,
  As Thou comest from above.

Rend our hearts in sorrow sighing,
  Stir our souls to seek for Thee;
Turn Thy wrath and meet our crying;
  Help us from our sin to flee.
There is none that seeketh rightly,
  Yet, O Father, we are Thine;
Come, O come, revive us quickly —
  Make our hearts to Thee incline.

Cause us now Thy way to cherish,
  And Thy righteousness to hold;
Hear our plea, Lord, else we perish!
  Call and bring us to Thy fold.
None hath seen so dear a Saviour;
  None hath heard so sweet a sound
As the name of our Redeemer:
  May His praises now abound.

## Revival and Restoration of the Church

Thou dost meet the heart that seeks Thee,
  Righteousness His robe and joy;
Thou delightest in Thy mercy
  When our souls Thy grace employ.
Since the world began its journey
  Eye and ear have never seen,
All the wonders of the glory
  God provides, beyond our dream.

Lord the sight of our condition,
  Degradation is our way;
Filthy garments our destruction,
  Sin would hold its evil sway.
Like a faded leaf we wither,
  Causèd by the wind to fly:
Brief our life and we can never
  Stay the hand that bids us die.

Cause us now to call upon Thee,
  Call upon the Name of Names;
Stir our hearts to gaze at Calvary,
  There behold reviving flames.
Holy gates of Zion City,
  Now let Israel see Thy face,
For the God of might and glory
  Dwells within Thy holy place.

# 94

*Then a cloud covered the tent of the congregation, and the glory
of the Lord filled the tabernacle. And Moses was not able to enter
the tent of the congregation, because the cloud abode thereon,
and the glory of the Lord filled the tabernacle.*

Exodus 40:34,35

(D.C.M.  Kingsfold)

O hear the cry of saints below,
    Although we are but few,
We long to see Thy mercy flow,
    And know Thy grace is true.
Almighty God, Redeemer King,
    Reveal Thy saving arm;
Display Thy majesty, and bring
    A myriad souls from harm.

O grant our hungry souls a sight
    Of glorious sovereign grace;
Yet clouds of mercy veil the light
    Of Jesu's smiling face.
O let Thy glory dress this tent,
    Our hearts with rapture fill
With certain hope, when Thou art bent
    Our longing hearts to thrill.

O leave us not in deep despair
    With dreaded word of loss;
Thy glory gone, and none to bear
    The tidings of Thy cross.
Revive Thy work, grant Thine embrace
    To us by day and night,
A shaft of fire, a cloud of grace:
    Display Thy word in might.

# 95

*The voice of him that crieth in the wilderness, Prepare ye the way of the Lord,
make straight in the desert a highway for our God.*

Isaiah 40:3

(10.10. 10.10. Pantyfedwyn)

The highway of the Lord hast thou not known?
Prepared by grace for men to find a way;
A path declared, His Gospel made renown:
The Prince of Glory takes our sin away.

*The valleys give their voices now to raise,
And mountains melt before Thy powerful name;
Good tidings come and Zion fills with praise
For God has come His Gospel to proclaim.*

The glory of the Lord is now revealed,
A voice has cried and all the earth hast heard
The message of the God in Christ who healed
The sorrow and the sin against His Word.

He fainteth not nor faileth in His love,
Yet youths shall fall in all their vanity;
But those who call and wait for Him above,
Like eagles rise and see His Calvary.

This is the God to whom all nations bend,
For time and space are nestled in His hand.
He is the Lord, and will the heavens rend
And blessing pour upon a thirsty land.

O comfort, comfort let there ever be
For He is God and ever reigns supreme;
Our sorrows banished by His love's decree,
O love of God, in Christ who doth redeem.

# 96

*If my people, which are called by my name, shall humble themselves, and pray,*
*and seek my face, and turn from their wicked ways; then will I hear from heaven,*
*and will forgive their sin, and will heal their land.*

2 Chronicles 7:14

(C.M. St. Fulbert)

Come let us praise that Holy Name,
  Loved and exalted high!
The name above all men and fame,
  That brings salvation nigh.

We are the people of His choice,
  Called by His holy name.
Help us to listen to His voice
  That takes away our shame.

Humble us now to pray and seek,
  The beauty of Thy face;
Grant that we ever shall be meek,
  Never Thy truth deface.

Turn us away from wicked ways,
  O Lord, we now implore;
Come to us quickly, with us stay,
  That we may Thee adore.

The land is healed when Thou dost touch
  Thy people with Thy hand;
Come quickly, Lord, our need is such,
  The grip of sin disband.

Happy the people who enjoy
  The precious presence sweet;
Happy the land that does employ
  Its days Thy name to greet.

# 97

*Turn us, O God of our salvation, and cause Thine anger toward us to cease.*

Psalm 85:4

(11.10. 11.10.  O Perfect Love)

Favour Thy land, O God of all creation,
O turn Thy fury from Thy chosen flock.
Captives of Judah, grant them Thy salvation;
Show forth Thy strength, Thou Everlasting Rock.

Oh cause Thine anger now to cease forever!
Forgive our sins and all our foolish way;
Revive Thy work, and never let us sever
From Thy dear self, O let us ever stay.

Speak peace unto Thy saints despite our failing;
Speak to us now and cause us to rejoice;
Teach us to long for blessing, on Thee calling;
Teach us to love and listen to Thy voice.

Mercy and truth, for ever met together,
Righteousness now has kissed the peace of grace.
Truth shall spring forth and bring the blessèd shower;
Then down from heaven reflect His radiant face.

Give what is good to every trembling nation,
Pity our plight without Thy living flame;
Step forth into this present generation:
Kindle a fire, revive, restore Thy Name.

# 98

*And I John saw the holy city, new Jerusalem, coming down from God out of heaven, prepared as a bride adorned for her husband.*

Revelation 21:2

(C.M. Hiraeth)

There is a home with God above,
A place of peace and joy;
A sweet inheritance of love
Which nothing can destroy.

At last my soul shall enter in
And join the happy throng;
'A ransom paid for all my sin'
Shall be my joy and song.

Such sacrifice of costly grace;
The Saviour died for me:
Enabled me to see His face,
To live eternally.

Surrounded by such loveliness,
My heart has lost all fear;
I see the Father's tenderness
Who wipes away each tear.

Time and decay shall reign no more,
For death has lost its sting.
The victor rules forevermore,
My Lord and glorious King.

The wonder of God's grace untold,
The mysteries of His will,
He tenderly will now unfold,
And show His sovereign skill.

The freedom of His presence gives
Each precious soul delight,
And happy is the soul that lives
To see this vision bright.

# 99

*Behold, how good and how pleasant it is for brethren to dwell together in unity!*

Psalm 133:1

(87.87.D.  Dim Ond Iesu)

Gaze upon the hills of Zion,
Rising in their strong array,
There the dew of gentle Hermon,
Springs with purity each day.
Sweet the incense of Thy freshness,
Sweet the presence of our King;
Glorious is Thy ready kindness,—
This Thy saints will ever sing.

Blessèd sight to see each brother,
Pleasant is their happy part;
One in Thee and in each other;
Blessèd unity of heart.
Like the kindness of God's favour
Shed in fragrance on their gown;
Blessèd garment of Thy splendour;
Sweet the incense of Thy dawn.

There the blessing God commanded;
There in hearts united, strong;
There the person of the Godhead;
Blessèd Saviour be their song.
Hail! all hail our blest Redeemer!
Hail, Thy coming now to stay;
Praise and glory be for ever,
Let Thy sceptre gently sway.

# 100

*And one shall say unto Him, What are these wounds in Thine hands? Then He shall answer, those with which I was wounded in the house of my friends.*

Zechariah 13:6

(C.M. Salzburg)

Awake O sword of Israel's Lord
And smite the Shepherd now:
According to Thy holy word,
Thou must Thy grace allow.

To wound Thy Son with hurt so sore
Yet rich in grace for men:
Our hearts will ever Thee adore,
And sing the sweet Amen.

Within the house of friends was He
Betrayed and crucified;
Yet in His death on Calvary
All hell He then defied.

He is the Rose of Sharon fair,
He is the Lily frail;
He is the Son beyond compare,
His grace shall never fail.

Lord Jesus Christ, we Thee acclaim,
Only Begotten Son;
Thy work, Thy death, Thy life, Thy fame,
Both heaven and earth have won.

# 101

*Turn us again, O God, and cause Thy face to shine; and we shall be saved.*

Psalm 80:3

(8.10.10.4. Ellasgarth)

Turn us again, Shepherd Divine;
  Cherubims praise and heaven declares Thy Name:
Name of Our Lord and name to us most dear;
  Kindle a flame.

Kindle a flame, within the hearts,
  Stir us to seek and turn to God again:
O let Thy grace draw forth our souls to Thee,
  Thy name to claim.

Teach us to weep for godly gifts;
  Tears in great measure grant to us today:
Tasting the bread, the sorrows of the Head,
  Whom men did slay.

O bless the fruit for it is Thine,
  Pour forth Thy presence, see our cruel foes;
Stir up Thy strength and come, O come O Lord!
  Remove our woes.

Jerusalem is desolate,
  Yet once was full with glory and with grace;
The shadow of Thy Cross spread through the land:
  We seek Thy face.

Look down upon Thy heritage;
  Let fruits of grace flow down as holy wine;
Revive Thy work, and cause Thine own to praise:
  Visit this vine!

# 102

*And let it be when Thou hearest the sound of a going in the tops*
*of the mulberry trees, that then thou shalt bestir thyself:*
*for then shall the Lord go out before thee...*

2 Samuel 5:24

(11.10.11.10.  O Perfect Love *or* Hold Thou my Hand)

What is this sound among the mulberry bushes?
What is this movement of Thy tender grace?
What is this sign that wondrous blessing ushers?
Who is this One with majesty of place?

Whence came this host with myriad voices praising?
Whence came the sound of melody so sweet?
This is the triumph, hear the angels singing
'Glory to God!' and fall before His feet.

Happy the throng, the breeze of heaven feeling;
Happy the hearts enveloped in Thy love.
Blessèd the hour of God's times of refreshing!
Windows of heaven that open from above.

These are the armies of the God of mercy,
Mighty in favour and sweeping all away;
No foe can stand or ever hope for glory —
His is the victory, so be it Lord alway.

# 103

*Wilt Thou not revive us again: that Thy people may rejoice in Thee?*

Psalm 85:6

(10.10.10.10. Toulon)

Revive Thy work, as in the days of yore,
    Stir up our souls and cause us to adore;
Stretch forth Thine arm and draw us to Thy fold:
    Forgotten be our foolish days of old.

Sweet is the favour that we now receive,
    Gentle the presence as we thus believe:
Visit Thy vineyard, grace to us incline,
    And let our praises be Thy sweetest vine.

Humble our hearts, and lift us to Thy throne,
    Cause us to cry and call on Thee alone.
Almighty Saviour, Lord, Redeemer, Friend;
    Thou art our Sovereign God and glorious end.

Blessèd the people that upon Thee call,
    Endless the blessing that our hearts enthrall:
Glory to God His majesty be praised,
    Incense of worship, evermore be raised.

# 104

Based on Isaiah 62.

(88.88.  Celeste)

The day of Thy grace is at hand
　To tell and to trust in Thy Name,
Thy righteousness stands to command
　Thine honour and glory and fame.

No more shall Jerusalem mourn,
　Nor heaviness wear them that weep;
His beauty for ashes will turn
　The contrite, their Saviour to greet.

The spirit of praise shall be heard
　In Zion, the city of God,
Proclaiming the truth of His Word,
　Good tidings their tongues sound abroad.

Forsaken, forgotten no more
　And stark desolation they spurn;
Delight of the Lord, O restore
　Her lamp of salvation to burn.

Prepare, O prepare for the day
　The glory of God will appear.
Prepare, O prepare now the way;
　Dispel from your hearts every fear.

O Sought out and cherished by grace,
　Go through, O go through His great gates,
And enter with worship, and raise
　His standard, and hold His dictates.

# THE CHRISTIAN LIFE

## 105

*For I have learned, in whatsoever state I am, therewith to be content.*

Philippians 4:11

(D.C.M.  St. Matthew)

Eternal Splendour, Glorious God,
   Thy gospel light so pure
Outshines the brilliance of the sun
   With grace that will endure.
My feeble efforts, failing life,
   I dare not offer Thee:
The merits of redeeming blood
   Are all sufficiency.

The raging torrents of the storm
   The boat of life submerge;
And all my strivings to survive
   Are buried in the surge.
The voice of Jesus bids me peace,
   And tells me He is nigh;
When I believe His presence true,
   It drives away my sigh.

The taunts of those who love Him not
   Sound loud within my heart;
So fears and fancies on me crowd,
   And I would fail my part.
In days of trial He has said
   That by my side He'll stand;
He'll not forsake, He'll not forget
   His vow to hold my hand.

## The Christian Life

In whatsoever state I am,
    For this I daily learn:
To be content, to be controlled
    By God's almighty arm.
He is the Lord that rides the storm,
    The One in death's dark hall;
Where'er I am, whate'er my lot,
    He is my all in all.

Sufficient is the grace of God
    To meet my every need;
Embracing is the love of Christ,
    And warms my heart indeed.
To glorious God, Eternal Son,
    Blest Spirit, sacred, sweet;
Honour and glory, praises give,
    Until at last we meet.

To gaze upon Thy beauty there,
    And see Thee as Thou art,
Will fill my mind, will feed my soul,
    And overwhelm my heart.
The mansions of the House of God
    No trouble can destroy;
The saints of Christ who dwell within
    Find endless peace and joy.

# 106

*Speaking to yourselves in psalms and hymns and spiritual songs, singing and making melody in your hearts to the Lord; giving thanks always for all things unto God and the Father in the name of our Lord Jesus Christ.*

Ephesians 5:19,20

(66.84.D.   Dolwyddelan)

With thankful heart I praise
The God who reigns supreme:
His providence and sweetest grace
    My constant theme.
The storm and wind may blow,
My life in turmoil be,
But I believe, and this I know —
    He pilots me.

Submissive to His will
Are land and sea and sky,
When He commands the waves are still,
    They hear His cry.
The Lord who shaped the earth,
And called a world to sight,
Who brought about a mighty birth,
    Is Lord of light.

I trust this Mighty One
Who took my guilt away;
He saw the suffering of His Son,
    My sin did slay.
What wondrous love I see
That took my shame and loss;
For Jesus Christ the penalty
    Paid on the Cross.

The Christian Life

Whatever life may hold
In joy or burden sad,
My God will all my time unfold,
    And make me glad.
He is the God of grace,
Who rules my span of life;
His sovereign power and sweet embrace
    Remove the strife.

All things are in His hand,
I thankfully rejoice;
His mercy grants me strength to stand,
    And heed His voice.
A song of joy within,
Inspired by Calvary —
This act divine my heart did win —
    Sweet melody.

# 107

*I waited patiently for the Lord; and he inclined unto me, and heard my cry.*
Psalm 40:1

(D.C.M.  Kingsfold)

I waited sadly for the Lord,
    But darkness veiled His face;
I clung to sin and shunned His Word;
    Yet longed to prove His grace.
A heavy burden on me lay
    And conflict tore my heart;
No satisfaction from each way;
    Despair was all my part.

## The Christian Life

The Lord inclined and heard my cry
    And saw my dreadful plight:
A path of sin and pit of clay,
    A place of dismal night.
He brought me out of unbelief,
    And showed me truth divine;
With quickening touch with life so brief,
    Immortal breath was mine.

My feet upon a rock I found,
    His blessing on life's race,
A song of joy with sweetest sound,
    A melody of grace.
I'll praise the God of Abraham,
    Who saw how I had roamed,
For worthy, worthy is the Lamb,
    Who on the cross atoned.

# 108

*And you hath He quickened who were dead in trespasses and sins;*
Ephesians 2:1
(C.M.  Godre'r Coed)

O Lord, Thy touch hath stirred my soul
    And caused my heart to love;
My quickened mind hath been made whole
    To seek those things above.

There is a path of thought so true
    That brings me to Thy throne,
And there my heart may mercy sue
    And claim Thy grace my own.

Eye hath not seen, nor ear hath heard
    Those things that Thou hast there:
For every promise of Thy word
    Awaits my soul to dare.

O why should I let sorrow reign,
    When such a God is mine,
Who gives to me and gives again,
    And tells me, 'Mine is thine'?

The riches He hath stored for me
    No measurement can tell;
For in the love of Calvary
    All with my God is well.

The Holy Spirit now hath taught
    My being to adore;
The blessings Jesus Christ hath wrought
    Shall cause my soul to soar.

# 109

*Unto you therefore which believe He is precious.*

1 Peter 2:7

(87.87.D.  Constance)

I have not seen Thy face, O Lord,
    Yet with my heart I love Thee;
For Thou hast plucked each tender cord
    With pleasing touch of mercy.
O Saviour, Lord, my King and Friend,
    I worship Thee with gladness;
And by Thy grace I will defend
    Thy Name that brought me kindness.

## The Christian Life

I have not known Thee here on earth,
　Yet with my soul I trust Thee;
For Thou hast stirred my thought to birth
　Of God and heaven and glory.
O precious Saviour, hear my praise
　With songs of joy and wonder;
For Thou hast taught my lips to raise
　A theme of words so tender.

Now I have seen Thy glorious face,
　With eyes of faith unveiling
The splendour of the theme of grace,
　All to my mind revealing.
Such bliss and happiness is mine
　To know the God of glory;
For who could call the Lord divine
　But for Thy grace and mercy?

# 110

*I will never leave thee, nor forsake thee.*
Hebrews 13:5
(98.98.D.  Crugybar)

I saw a new vision of Jesus,
　A view I'd not seen here before,
Beholding in glory so wondrous
　With beauty I had to adore.
I stood on the shores of my weakness,
　And gazed at the brink of such fear;
'Twas then that I saw Him in newness,
　Regarding Him fair and so dear.

My Saviour will never forsake me,
    Unveiling His merciful face,
His presence and promise almighty,
    Redeeming His loved ones by grace.
In shades of the valley's dark terror,
    Where hell and its horror hold sway,
My Jesus will reach out in power,
    And save me by His only way.

For yonder a light shines eternal,
    Which spreads through the valley of gloom;
Lord Jesus, resplendent and regal,
    Drives fear far away from the tomb.
Our God is the end of the journey,
    His pleasant and glorious domain;
For there are the children of mercy,
    Who praise Him for Calvary's pain.

# 111

*Against Thee, Thee only have I sinned,*
*and done this evil in Thy sight.*

Psalm 51:4

(D.S.M. Llanllyfni)

Against Thee have I sinned,
    Before the King Divine,
And all my evil is exposed
    Before my eyes and Thine.
O hear me as I cry,
    Have mercy on my soul;
I come to Thee, O hear my sigh,
    Forgive and make me whole.

# The Christian Life

There is no worthiness
    Within my broken heart,
My fallen nature, sore distress
    Shall surely be my part;
Unless Thy grace lays hold
    With glorious truth to share
And grants me mercy to be bold
    When Thou hast shown Thy care.

Create, O God, within
    A heart both pure and clean;
Restore my spirit, blot my sin,
    And let me on Thee lean.
Thy Holy Spirit give —
    O never take away!
And grant that He may in me live,
    To give me joy this day.

Thy presence is my light —
    O never leave Thine own!
But fill my breast with pure delight
    That I am Thine alone.
O take my lips this day,
    Thy wonders to proclaim,
To tell of Thy redeeming way,
    And magnify Thy fame.

What dost Thou ask of me,
    What sacrifice to please?
For nothing in my hands can be
    Sufficient to appease.
O look upon my heart,
    Now broken, Lord, by grace;
My contrite spirit will not part,
    I'll ever seek Thy face.

# 112

*Put on the whole armour of God,*
*that ye may be able to stand against the wiles of the devil.*

Ephesians 6:11

(88.88.88.  Pater Omnium)

Armour of God, blest panoply,
My comfort, strength and mantle be:
Child of Thy grace redeemed by blood —
Saved from Thy wrath and Satan's flood.
Merit of Christ so rich and free
Pardons my sin and covers me.

With agile swiftness Satan's head
Is raised to strike, instilling dread:
A lion's roar or angel call
Are sent by him to make us fall.
Christian, awake! and cry to God,
Be amply girt and fully shod.

We wrestle hard and struggle long;
Christ and His strength to us belong.
Each moment of our pilgrimage
Is filled with danger, Satan's rage.
His wiles are subtle, sharp and wise;
We cry to Christ that we might rise.

Armour of God, O cover me,
With gospel truth my gown to be;
Imputed righteousness divine
My heart protects, I know He's mine.
My wandering feet in peaceful way,
Thy shield of faith for my array.

## The Christian Life

O take my mind, my blessèd Lord,
With helmet pure in thought and word:
Thy Word of God a sword of flame
So sharp and true, expounds the Name
Of Jesus Christ, the Son of Man
And Son of God, eternal span.

I pray to Thee, blest Trinity,
To God's Almighty Unity;
Thy sovereign rule I would adore,
And prove Thy power of boundless store.
Thy word can stay the Evil One,
A smile renew from Thy dear Son.

# 113

*I will liken him unto a wise man, which built his house upon a rock.*
Matthew 7:24

(D.C.M.  St. Matthew *or* Land of Rest *or* Seraph)

There is a Rock on which I stand
    And now I am secure;
Its mighty base within the land
    Of God's eternal shore.
It never moves, it never falls,
    Or fails to keep each saint
Who trusts in Christ, and on Him calls
    When Satan bids him faint.

Upon this Rock I now will build
    My life, and live for Thee;
O daily grant my vessel filled
    With Thy serenity.
A heart of prayer, a loving way
    That will not Jesus fail;
So grace may flow to those who stray,
    And see Thy love prevail.

## The Christian Life

What is this Rock, this place of peace,
   Above the fears of life,
That grants me joy and gives me grace
   To live above the strife?
This Rock is Christ of Calvary
   Who took away my stain,
Whose life and death avail for me;
   Eternal life I gain.


# 114

*I count all things but loss for the excellency
of the knowledge of Christ Jesus my Lord.*

Philippians 3:8

(L.M.  Bodmin)

I once believed my life a gain,
And thought that I would grace attain:
The Spirit showed me all the dross,
And now I see it all but loss.

Then I beheld the Saviour's face,
And looked upon a life of grace:
When I compared my feeble chart,
Shame and remorse then filled my heart.

O to be found in Christ alone,
For on the cross He did atone:
He took my sin and nailed it there,
And gave a gown of grace to wear.

Now I dismiss my foolish pride,
Covered in Christ, in whom I hide:
All this by faith that will not fail,
Granted by God, I will prevail.

## The Christian Life

O wondrous joy the Lord to know,
I will delight Thy name to show:
Yet, I desire to know Thee more,
I hunger for Thy boundless store.

Thy risen power I long to prove,
Fully enabled in each move:
Through fellowship of suffering sweet,
I worship Thee and ever greet.

Confirm me now in image strange;
Death worketh life, what great exchange!
Yet I believe in Thine increase;
Lord, evermore may I decrease.

Lord, all my life to do Thy will,
This by Thy grace I will fulfill:
Then Thou wilt change my body vile,
Fashioned in Christ — I wait awhile.

# 115

*They that sow in tears shall reap in joy.*
Psalm 126:5

(C.M.  Hiraeth)

When in an alien land we wept
    And sang Thy praises there,
Sad was our song, yet we were kept
    Safe in Thy gracious care.

Far, far away we kept Thy word
    And cherished Thy dear name;
We heeded not the scorn and sword
    Of those who Thee defame.

## The Christian Life

Thy precious seed of life we bore
  Sowing in tears of love;
Longing to see that open door
  With blessings from above.

Often we dreamt of Thy great power,
  And agonized in prayer;
Then in Thy mercy came a shower
  Of grace upon us there.

The people trembled at the sound
  Of such a God as Thee;
Then Thou didst come, and we were found
  Safe in Thine arms to be.

Our mouths were filled with laughter loud
  And song in sweet accord,
Then with our hearts and souls we bowed
  To Thee our sovereign God.

Many the sheaves our arms did raise
  Of those by Thee embraced;
Thine be the glory, ours the praise
  As we Thy wonders traced.

Like those that dream and yet awake
  We dreamt of being free;
For now in Christ the captives break
  Their bonds in Calvary.

# 116

*Receiving the end of your faith, even the salvation of your souls.*

1 Peter 1:9

(66.66.88.  St. John)

Enable me to see
  By faith my heavenly home,
A land of love to me,
  Secured by grace alone:
For God Himself will wipe away
All tears of pain and death's decay.

Enable me to know
  The depths of Thine embrace;
The hope of heaven below,
  Inheritance of grace:
For God is good in all His ways
And every promise love displays.

Enable me to live
  Believing in Thy word,
What e'er my lot will give
  My heart Thy truth has heard.
Forever has Thy truth maintained
A myriad souls in His domain.

Enable me to feel
  That Thou art ever near.
I at Thy throne appeal
  And ever will appear;
For there Thy mercy I obtain,
Until my soul shall heaven attain.

Enable me to love,
　　O God of love, Thy Son;
Graced by Thy Holy Dove,
　　The love that makes us one:
That I may know and love for Thee,
Beneath the cross of Calvary.

# 117

*Verily, verily, I say unto you, Except a corn of wheat fall into the ground and die,
it abideth alone: but if it die, it bringeth forth much fruit.*

John 12:24

(C.M.  St. Stephen)

A corn of wheat abides alone,
　　Except it fall and die;
Deep in the ground new life is born,
　　Yet there it has to lie.

Deep in the mystery of grace
　　Of Thine eternal realm,
Thy blessèd Son took our disgrace,
　　And thus fulfilled Thy plan.

Death worketh life on Calvary,
　　And sinner's burden borne;
A place for man from wrath to flee,
　　The Saviour's crown adorn.

We gaze upon an empty cross,
　　And on a gaping grave:
The Saviour died, yet in His loss,
　　Eternal life He gave.

## The Christian Life

Until we die to self and sin,
    Then we abide alone;
Yet when we die we live in Him,
    And stand before that throne.

Death worketh life — O image strange!
    Life that shall endless be,
Exquisite truth and sweet exchange —
    Thy gift at Calvary.

# 118

*To appoint unto them that mourn in Zion, to give unto them beauty for ashes,*
*the oil of joy for mourning, the garment of praise for the spirit of heaviness;*
*that they might be called trees of righteousness, the planting of the Lord,*
*that He might be glorified.*

Isaiah 61:3

(C.M.  Bangor)

Thy beauty Lord for ashes give
    To those who mourn for Thee;
Their hearts desire, for Thee to live;
    Their utmost: Christ to see.

The oil of joy, Thy Spirit's grace,
    O grant and pour on Thine;
For those that long to see Thy face,
    And taste heaven's sweetest wine.

The broken heart Thou dost restore,
    And set the captive free:
The riches of Thy boundless store,
    Displayed at Calvary.

## The Christian Life

The garment of Thy righteousness,
   Bring praises from the heart;
A path of grace and holiness,
   Be now our pleasant part.

Thy beauty Lord, that day behold,
   In fulness of Thy joy;
The praises of Thy name untold,
   Of grace Thou didst employ.

The garment of Thy blessèd Son,
   Shall robe our waiting frame;
For evermore to be Thine own,
   And dwell in halls of fame.

# 119

*As the hart panteth after the water brooks,*
*so panteth my soul after Thee, O God.*

Psalm 42:1

(D.C.M.  St. Leonard's)

O Lord, Thou seest my distress,
   Loud waves have covered me:
The depths of ocean on me press,
   And from false friends I flee.
Yet in my heart desires I find;
   With breathless pant I cast
My lonely soul on God so kind;
   Sad tears are my repast.

With soul cast down, men's jibes did smart,
   And filled my cup with pain.
I worshipped Thee with empty heart,
   I yearned for Thee again.

Remembrance came, that God of yore
    Displayed past care to me;
With reassurance that the store
    Was boundless as the sea.

My weary soul upon Him gazed;
    His love was none the less:
Before the truth I stood amazed,
    His glorious faithfulness.
For now I saw with startled look
    The Rock beneath my feet;
This firm foundation never shook,
    Nor ever knew defeat.

I'll praise my God with new delight,
    My countenance and health;
My mourning change for gown of light,
    Rejoice in Jesus' wealth.
The name of Christ now fills my heart
    With His security:
My blessèd Lord will not depart,
    His promise covers me.

# 120

*For ye have not received the spirit of bondage again to fear;*
*but ye have received the Spirit of adoption whereby we cry, Abba, Father.*

Romans 8:15

(88.88.88.  Rhyd-y-Groes)

Sad were our chains and sore unkind,
Heirs of the Fall, to sin inclined;
Dark were our hearts, and dim our sight,
No ray of light to pierce our night:
The Son of God with mighty key
Opened the gate to set us free.

## The Christian Life

Wonderful Saviour, Prince of Peace,
Almighty Hand, who did release
Many a soul in sore distress
With heavy load of wickedness;
For Thou hast granted peace of mind,
A tranquil heart from God so kind.

Heirs of salvation, costly price,
Spirit Divine, who did entice;
Merits of Christ to us applied,
In whose glad hearts assurance cried;
Joint heirs with Christ, dispelling fear —
Spirit of bondage, disappear!

When we beheld the Saviour's face,
He who was nailed for man's disgrace,
We stood amazed at such a feat,
To see the Victor hell defeat.
Loud hallelujahs ring the sky,
For God has heard the sinner's cry.

# 121

*And the Lord turned, and looked on Peter*

Luke 22:61

(86.84.  St. Cuthbert)

There is a place of sweet repose,
  A rest upon the way,
A shelter from a myriad foes:
  In Thee my stay.

I hide secure beside this Tree,
  A place of curse and shame,
Where Thou hast wrought a victory:
  A glorious flame.

## The Christian Life

Now I shall dwell for ever here
    Whatever may befall,
In life and death, in every sphere:
    Thy grace my all.

In all my life Thou dost impart
    The gifts of love and care;
Yet sweeter far is what Thou art,
    Beyond compare.

But there are times I wander far,
    And from Thy side depart;
I turn away, Thy work to mar
    And grieve Thy heart.

What low desires within my breast
    That pierce Thy wounds afresh,
And follow still what I detest —
    Deceitful flesh!

O keep me, Lord, beneath Thy wing,
    For ever sheltered there
From Satan and his evil sting,
    My Saviour fair.

# 122

*O Lord, Thou hast searched me, and known me.*

Psalm 139:1

(C.M.  Bishopthorpe)

All that I am I now confess,
    And let Thy gaze explore
The hidden depths which so distress
    And daily I deplore.

## The Christian Life

When painful light I welcome now,
 Revealing all my sin;
I cry for mercy, as I bow
 My heart for Thee to win.

I know Thou art a God supreme:
 O hear my heart implore,
For in my mind I fondly dream
 Of grace that will restore.

Restore my soul, my heart refresh
 In avenues of peace,
Where grace and truth on mortal flesh
 Are gifts God will release.

All that I am now thrills in Thee,
 The Lord and Judge of all;
For I have heard at Calvary
 The sweetest heavenly call.

# 123

*That I may know Him, and the power of His resurrection, and the fellowship
of His sufferings, being made conformable unto His death.*
Philippians 3:10

(D.C.M.  St. Matthew)

Deep in my heart there is a sigh,
 A longing, Lord, for Thee;
To know the depths that in Thee lie,
 The grace of Calvary.
O grant that I might understand
 Thy glorious mystery,
More of Thyself, and by Thy hand
 Obedience stir in me.

# The Christian Life

Thy living power I long to prove
    In resurrection might,
With overcoming grace to move
    Each sin that dims this light.
O grant that I may find the source
    Of hidden strength and stay,
Which flows from Thee, and on its course
    O draw my soul each day.

There is a fellowship of pain
    Deep in Thy heart of love,
Of suffering sweet, eternal gain,
    The tears of heaven above.
O grant me, Lord, to feel this joy,
    These tremors of Thy grace;
Engraved by Thee, none can destroy
    The riches I embrace.

Then lead me in this wondrous way
    To die to self and sin;
And take me, Lord, when Thou dost slay,
    And drive Thy grace within.
O grant me now an image sweet
    Impressed upon my heart;
With joy I lie beneath Thy feet,
    To weep and not depart.

# 124

*In my Father's house are many mansions: if it were not so,*
*I would have told you. I go to prepare a place for you…*

John 14:2

(86.84.  St. Cuthbert)

How sweet the knowledge in my heart
  Of mansions fair above,
Where Thou, my Saviour, ever art,
  O fount of love.

This transient world with sorrows deep,
  And pain, and grief and woe,
Shall be no more, so none shall weep
  Or fear the foe.

The sting of death, removed by grace
  Can never harm us there,
For we are safe in His embrace
  Above all fear.

My longing soul is satisfied
  For Jesus Christ is mine;
My thirst is quenched, my hunger filled
  With meat divine.

My faith is turned to glorious sight
  As I my Lord behold;
My hope fulfilled, I see His might—
  His power untold.

He gave me love, and on its course
  He drew me to His breast,
And there I saw the fount and source
  Where love does rest.

## The Christian Life

Forever with the Lord to be,
    A pardoned sinner now;
A promise realised to me—
    His perfect vow.


# 125

*Why art thou cast down, O my soul? and why art thou disquieted within me?*
*hope thou in God: for I shall yet praise Him,*
*who is the health of my countenance, and my God.*

Psalm 42:11

(C.M.  Hiraeth)

When storms of life engulf my way,
    And sorrows crowd my breast,
One thought prevails, and is my stay —
    Thy providence is best.

Unmoveable, Thy providence
    Remains secure and still,
Provides the grace for my defence
    In face of every ill.

Why does my soul within me fear?
    Why does my heart grow cold?
When in Thy sight I am most dear;
    Such love should make me bold.

Thy mercies past have never failed,
    Nor has Thy goodness waned;
Thy faithful kindness has prevailed,
    Thy will has always reigned.

## The Christian Life

Thy person and Thy work remain
In perfect harmony;
Unswerving in Thy purpose plain,
Thy providence to me.

Come all my foes to crush my heart,
Come Satan's host to kill;
Then come my Lord to take my part
My cup with joy to fill.

In every place I'll praise Thy name,
And never doubt Thy care;
Thy providence remains the same,
For Thou art always there.

# 126

*That Christ may dwell in your hearts by faith; that ye, being rooted and grounded in love, may be able to comprehend with all saints what is the breadth, and length, and depth, and height; and to know the love of Christ, which passeth knowledge, that ye might be filled with all the fulness of God.*

Ephesians 3:17,18,19

(10.10.10.10. Pantyfedwen)

O grant on earth the knowledge in my heart,
That springs in heaven and gives my soul a part
In His redemption, cleansing all my sin,
Enlightens me and brings me safe within.

*O rich redemption, plentitude of grace,*
*That paid the penalty of my disgrace;*
*Only begotten Son of God has won*
*Through His eternal Spirit made us one.*

# The Christian Life

O let me know the vastness of Thy store,
That my desire may ever be for more,
And let Thy grasp now firmly grip my soul,
For my great Saviour sought and made me whole.

O let me feel Thy Christ within me dwell,
Applying faith that doeth all things well;
With all my heart, O let the heavens rend
And show me now my long expected end.

O flood my heart, and fill my life with praise,—
To Thee above shall holy anthems raise;
O fill me now, my inner man renew,
To know and feel Thy heart's refreshing dew.

Enough for me to know that I am Thine,
And yet the greater gift, that Thou art mine:
The living God belong to such as I,
By grace, I dare to utter such a cry!

O let me taste the love of God to live,
Shed in its fulness—only His to give;
O let His presence now my portion be,
To glimpse the depths of Thine infinity!

Almighty God, Thou art the heavenly source,
Of peace and love to which I find recourse.
Untiring in my Lord alone for Thee,
Unfailing in my love for Calvary.

Kept by Thy grace, commanded by Thy love,
No foe I fear, as anchored safe above,
Past hell's dark empire, Thou hast paved a way
For me to come and ever with Thee stay.

# 127

*Behold the days come, saith the Lord, that I will make a new covenant
with the house of Israel, and with the house of Judah.*

Jeremiah 31:31

(88.88.D.  Trewen)

I gaze at the wonder of love
My God has unfolded to me;
A love that will plan from above,
A guide that will lead me to Thee.

*The grace of Thy covenant care,*
*Entrances my soul with delight;*
*For Thou art the God who dost share*
*Thy riches of grace in my sight.*

The things that would bring me dismay,
I lay in Thy wonderful hands;
That maketh all things in Thy way
To serve and obey Thy demands.

The sorrows of guilt and of sin
Forever are taken away.
Thy grace is my comfort within;
Thy word is my strength in that day.

Secure in Thy love I remain,
For no separation can be;
My Saviour forever will reign—
The victor of blest Calvary.

# 128

*My grace is sufficient for thee: for My strength is made perfect in weakness.*

2 Corinthians 12:9

(D.C.M.  Ellacombe *or* Kingsfold)

Thy tender grace I've sought so long,
  Thy gentle touch to feel;
To know within my heart a song
  Thy mercy will reveal.
O gaze upon my aching soul,
  And hasten to restore;
O tell me Thou canst make me whole,
  Cause me to love Thee more.

What are the hindrances in me
  That turn my gaze away,
And make my soul to flee from Thee
  Who art my hope and stay?
Thy Spirit showed me depths within
  Of deep rebellious ways,
And taught me more about my sin
  By His exposing rays.

O rouse my soul to call on Thee
  On whom my sin was laid;
Remind my heart of Calvary
  Where my great debt was paid.
How could I ever Thee forget,
  Or roam from Thy dear side?
Forgive me, Lord, for my neglect;
  In Thee let me abide.

The Christian Life

At last my soul in Thee hath found
  All, all sufficient grace,
And I shall be in mercy bound,
  And dwell in Thine embrace.
I'll seek Thee more, and find Thee still
  All Thou hast claimed to be;
O grant that now, unhindered, will
  Thy grace fill even me.

# 129

*But they that wait upon the Lord shall renew their strength;*
*they shall mount up with wings as eagles;*
*they shall run, and not be weary; they shall walk and not faint.*

Isaiah 40:31

(D.C.M.  Seraph)

Comfort our hearts, our strength renew,
  And give us power to stand;
Our length of days with grace endue,
  And guide us by Thy hand.
When we are faint and full of fear
  And Satan presses sore,
We know our Lord will always hear
  And aid us from His store.

Thou dost revive all them that wait
  Upon the Lord of life;
The grace of eagles is their flight,
  Surmounting every strife.
For Thou dost give the power to run
  The race before us planned;
A steadfast walk now has begun,
  A way Thou dost demand.

Have we not known, have we not seen
   Thy pleasant, glorious reign?
The young men falter, faint and fall,
   For all their strength is vain.
Thou Lord of all the earth and sky,
   Supreme in all Thy ways,
Our Great Defender, hear our cry,
   And guide us all our days.

# 130

*The eyes of your understanding being enlightened.*

Ephesians 1:18

(S.M.  Bod Alwyn)

Lord, open Thou my eyes,
   Wonderful grace to see,
Where Jesus Christ is nailed and dies
   There on a hill for me.

Lord, open Thou my mind,
   More of Thy wealth to know;
Furnish my life with grace so kind
   From Thine abundant flow.

Lord, open Thou my heart;
   Graciously now enfold;
Stir up my love and never part
   From this eternal hold.

Lord, open Thou my hand
   To take Thy grace as mine,
That in that day in Christ I'll stand
   In righteousness divine.

Lord, Thou hast touched my soul,
    Thy gentle hand I feel;
With healing that has made me whole,
    Thy grace did o'er me steal.

Praise to Thy name, O Lord,
    Wondrous, immortal Three!
Now I shall sing in sweet accord
    Wonderful grace in me.

# 131

*Saw ye Him whom my soul loveth?*
Song of Solomon 3:3
(D.C.M.  Rhos *or* Vox Dilecti)

When God approached, my foolish heart
    Withdrew and turned away;
I caused the Saviour to depart,
    And this my peace did slay.
What cold indifference chilled my soul
    Which cast me from His breast?
I learned anew the heavy toll
    Of sin and sad distress.

What great alarm crept through my frame
    That drove me to my feet,
To search for Jesus in my shame,
    And seek His grace so sweet!
My panting soul lamented now
    Such apathy and sin;
I longed before my Lord to bow,
    And bring my grief to Him.

## The Christian Life

He must have known my deep desire
    To draw me to His side;
My yearning yielded fiercer fire:
    With Him I must abide.
My anxious lips endeared His name,
    Proclaimed His grace to all;
Yet for myself I could not claim
    This joy within my soul.

He heard my heart cry out in pain
    To feel His presence pure;
His wondrous form appeared again
    With love that will endure.
I call Him mine, but I am His
    With covenant of grace,
For now I know that heaven's kiss
    Is seen in Jesu's face.

Amongst the roses of the earth
    My Saviour is supreme;
The lily white, despairs its worth,
    Such beauty cannot dream.
He is the fairest to my soul,
    My everlasting King;
He gives me grace, He makes me whole;
    My heart with joy will sing.

# 132

*Out of the depths have I cried unto Thee, O Lord. Lord, hear my voice:*
*let Thine ears be attentive to the voice of my supplications.*

Psalm 130:1,2

(88.88.88.  Surrey *or* Pater Omnium)

O soul of mine, what do I find,
　　This sudden sorrow and despair?
What shades of sadness so unkind,
　　To mar my joy and fill with care?
Surely Thy grace sufficient is,
Embrace my soul with heaven's kiss.

O heart of mine, call out for aid
　　From dismal depths and shadows deep;
Thy love extends and cannot fade,
　　Ever the same, with power to keep.
Surely I know from days of yore,
Thine ear is turned as I implore.

O Saviour mine, for evermore
　　Source of all comfort to my soul;
There is no limit to Thy store,
　　I'll prove Thy name whate'er befall.
God of all might and power, uphold
My fainting spirit, make me bold.

O joy of mine, with gaze from Thee,
　　Now fills my life in every sphere;
Twin gifts of faith and love to be
　　For ever joined in union here.
Beautiful grace Thou dost endow,
Heart, soul and will before Thee bow.

# 133

*What shall we say then to these things? If God be for us, who can be against us?*

Romans 8:31

(66.84.D.   Dolwyddelan)

What fierce and fearful foe
Surrounds my soul to slay?
When Satan comes with voice of woe
    In bold array.
My strength is in the Lord,
His armour covers me;
For God is for us, and His sword
    Is victory.

Now Sinai's voice I heard
That shattered all my pride;
On startling slate with piercing word;
    I could not hide.
My hope is in the grace
Of Jesus' righteousness,
For God is for us, His embrace
    Removes distress.

On Jordan's silent shore
I find I cannot live;
This cruel death a moment more
    Will never give.
O resurrection life,
This glorious living breath!
For God is for us, in the strife,
    The end of death.

All, all is now exposed
On dreadful judgement day;
But Jesus Christ has interposed
    That I might stay.

His blood is peace to me,
A place for me has bought;
For God is for us, glorious plea,
In all Christ wrought.

# 134

*The sacrifices of God are a broken spirit: a broken and a contrite heart,*
*O God, Thou wilt not despise.*

Psalm 51:17

(C.M.  Dundee *or* French)

O tell me, Lord, what pleaseth Thee:
Is there an offering meet?
For in my heart I long to see
Thy smile of grace so sweet.

Search as I may in all my way
And all my work and toil,
I cannot find a worthy day
That sin has failed to soil.

This heart of mine with depths profound
Yields disappointment keen,
And every effort I have found
Has leaned to self and sin.

Then I beheld the purest One,
With heart of love and peace,
Who shed His blood, a victory won,
And floods of joy release.

My heart is broken at the sight
Of such humility;
I stand amazed and bathe in light
Of this new dignity.

Now I can see my life is vain,
Contrition breaks my heart;
For now I know and feel the pain
That sin and shame impart.

Yet in some strange and wondrous way
This breaking pleaseth Thee;
For Thou wilt not despise or slay
A holy sorrow's plea.

I feel Thy smile upon my face,
And I rejoice to know
The blessèd bliss of Thine embrace
In lifting one so low.

# 135

*I am the door: by Me if any man enter in, he shall be saved,
and shall go in and out, and find pasture.*

John 10:9

(88.88.88.  St. Catherine)

Thy gentle hand has touched my heart
With quickening life Thou didst impart;
I never knew such grace could be,
Or joy and peace from Calvary.
Amazing grace, eternal Lord,
This life abundant spread abroad.

Thy gentle hand has touched my life,
Leading me onwards through the strife;
Comfort and strength for daily needs;
Thy wondrous presence now me leads.
In life or death or sore distress
I rest on Thy great faithfulness.

Thy gentle hand has touched my soul,
And brought me to Thy chosen fold,
Never to lose my way again,
Or wander in the paths of pain.
Now I rejoice in ways of grace,
Happy to see and know Thy face.

# 136

*There remaineth therefore a rest to the people of God.*

Hebrews 4:9

(D.S.M.  Nearer Home)

There is a rest prepared
    That we may enter in,
A place of peace where love has cared
    And dealt with all our sin.
The power of hell is stayed;
    The path of life is shown;
The dreadful penalty is paid:
    For sin did Christ atone.

There is a path prepared,
    Paved by the grace of heaven,
A place of joy and mercy shared,
    And sheltered from all harm.
We rest our weary souls,
    We cast our burdens here;
And find that Jesus Christ controls,
    Is King in every sphere.

There is a peace prepared,
　That silences the storm,
When all the elements have raged
　And left our souls forlorn.
This peace will now abide
　And drive away our fears;
Then draw us to Thy blessèd side,
　And wipe away our tears.

There is a place prepared,
　And Thou wilt bring us in;
Crush unbelief where sin has dared
　To enter such a scene.
O place our faith secure,
　And tell us we are blessed;
O grant a vision to endure,
　Our final Sabbath rest.


# 137

*O taste and see that the Lord is good:*
*blessed is the man that trusteth in Him.*

Psalm 34:8

(D.C.M.　Noel)


O stir my soul to gaze on Thee,
　Thou glorious King of light;
And bring my heart to Calvary,
　This strange and wondrous sight.
I long to know Thee as Thou art,
　O lead me now this day,
In such a way I shall not part,
　Nor ever from Thee stray.

What is the pain I now behold,
  Profound, with bitter taste,
Though planned afar in realms untold,
  Performed by men in haste?
Yet by some miracle of grace
  A sweetness fills my breast,
For death in Thee brings life's embrace,
  Eternal, pardoning rest.

Wake up, my hovering soul, to know
  The dangers that surround,
The myriad foes, death's final blow,
  And hell for those not found.
Send mercy, Lord, both swift and sure,
  And move this heart of stone
To touch Thy garment and the cure
  That comes from Thee alone.

# 138

*Set your affections on things above, not on things on the earth.*
Colossians 3:2

(D.C.M.  Castle Rising)

Wean my sad heart from things on earth;
  From deep rebellion draw
My disobedience and the dearth
  In me of all Thy law.
Show me the beauty of Thy Son—
  Immortal, born in time;
Salvation to my soul who won,
  And brought me peace sublime.

## The Christian Life

O guide me into depths of light
    To know and feel Thy gaze,
When pardon flows and moves the night,
    And sets my soul ablaze.
A saving hope within me now,
    A beacon on a hill,
The rays of Calvary endow
    The joy of heaven still.

Set my affections now on high
    To seek things that are Thine,
A holy hunger and a cry
    To call on the Divine.
O teach me how to feed on Thee,
    To live upon Thy word,
And prove the vast resourceful sea
    Thou hast for me reserved.

Cause the desires of my heart
    To long for Thee alone,
And in my mind a seeking start
    With Thee upon the throne.
Control and guide with tender touch
    My frailty, with Thy care;
In realms of grace I long so much
    To dwell, and glory share.

# 139

*For we are unto God a sweet savour of Christ.*

2 Corinthians 2:15

(88.88.88. St. Chrysostom)

Savour of Christ, possess my soul,
Mercy and joy upon me roll,
Like mighty waves of oceans fair,
With swell and surge above all care:
Sweetest Redeemer, Saviour, Friend,
'Tis only Thou this grace can send.

Influence my heart and fill my breast
With sweet aroma of the blest;
Fragrance of grace Thou dost afford
To spread Thine unction on Thy word:
Grant me such earnest from above,
Assure my heart that Thou art love.

Passion of Christ in suffering rude,
Prevail upon me, for He stood
Before Thy wrath and took my stain,
And bore the penalty and pain:
God of all glory, rich in grace,
O set my heart to seek Thy face!

# 140

*He died for all, that they which live should not henceforth live unto themselves,*
*but unto Him which died for them and rose again.*

2 Corinthians 5:15

(D.C.M.  St. Matthew)

What caused my heart to turn away
    From Thee, the Holy One;
And ever live for self-display,
    Delight in sin alone?
It was my pride whose haughty head
    Denied that I should bow;
Yet in my soul a sudden dread
    Appeared, I know not how.

It was a work ordained in heaven,
    Conceived by sovereign plan,
Redemption sweet for fallen men;
    And yet from God I ran.
Restoring grace laid hold on me,
    And turned my gaze to know
The horrors of the law, to see
    The sorrows I did sow.

O Holy Spirit, what is this
    Which shows a ransom paid,
A debt removed, this work of His
    The Son of God has made?
I live in Him who purchased me,
    And in His grace am found;
Now to this cross of Calvary
    I am for ever bound.

# 141

*I beseech you therefore, brethren, by the mercies of God,*
*that ye present your bodies a living sacrifice,*
*holy, acceptable unto God, which is your reasonable service.*

Romans 12:1

(C.M.  Dunfermline *or* Mendip)

Reach out my soul to Him who loves
    With powerful, pardoning grace.
Who touches me, my guilt removes,
    And gives my soul its place.

Reach out my heart to Him who cares
    And gives me life again,
Who lifts me up and now declares
    That I may heaven attain.

Reach out my life and let it be
    Transformed in service true;
O touch my days now filled with Thee,
    To give my Lord His due.

My soul, my heart, my days I give
    And live for Thee alone.
O bless this pittance and forgive,
    Yet it is all thine own.

# 142

*And He hath put a new song in my mouth, even praise unto our God: many shall see it and fear, and shall trust in the Lord.*

Psalm 40:3

(C.M. Southwell)

I find within my soul a sigh
    That nought on earth can meet:
I come to Thee, O Lord most high
    And with my heart Thee greet.

How can I come to Thee and live
    Except Thou draw me nigh,
And from Thy bounteous store do give
    The grace no more to die?

Thy Cross of mercy shows a way
    That God in love displays;
Where Thy dear Son has moved away
    My guilt, and peace has made.

I thank Thee for the grace that sought
    My weary soul for Thee,
And from the depths of sin has brought
    Me safe to Calvary.

How can I ever follow Thee
    With faltering steps and will,
If Thou wilt not enable me,
    And be my Guardian still?

Without Thy grace I cannot move,
    Nor holiness desire;
But now I find desires to prove
    And after Thee enquire.

Thou art the God who quickened me
And brought me from the dead,
Who causes me from sin to flee,
And live for Thee instead.

# 143

*I will lift up mine eyes unto the hills, from whence cometh my help.*

Psalm 121:1

(D.S.M.  Diademata)

Lift up mine eyes to seek
Thy face, O Saviour fair,
To see the beauty of the meek,
Thy glory to declare.
Such beauty robed with pain
Adorned the cross with grace,
A ransom paid, O sweet refrain,
Beloved, blessèd face.

Lift up my heart to find
Thy love of purest worth;
With sweet compassion for mankind
Embrace a son of earth.
To gaze upon that hill
Where love lit up a world,
To spread the grace of God until
All His are in the fold.

Lift up my soul to praise
The wonders of Thy name,
Of gospel truth, and thus to raise
The banner of Thy fame.
O sound salvation clear!
The dead stir to their feet,
And break the bonds of death and fear;
Thy word is hell's defeat.

# 144

*Lord, I believe; help Thou mine unbelief.*

Mark 9:24

(D.S.M.  From Strength to Strength)

What pangs of pain are these
　　That wound my troubled mind,
Which tell me of my soul's disease
　　And peace I cannot find?
My quickened conscience wakes,
　　And fills me with remorse,
For every way my life now takes,
　　My sin obscures my course.

O Lord, I had not known
　　My actions caused Thy grief,
If Mercy had not swiftly flown,
　　Displaying unbelief.
Such agony of heart,
　　To be estranged from Thee,
In endless darkness to depart,
　　Thy glory never see.

O touch of healing balm
　　That came from Calvary,
Through merit of this blood came calm
　　With wondrous peace to me.
O hush my heart within
　　And dwell in Jesu's fold;
Now evermore delight in Him,
　　See wonders yet untold.

# 145

*Is there no balm in Gilead?*

Jeremiah 8:22

(L.M.  Holley *or* Hamburg)

What wounds are these within my breast,
What holy sorrow and distress?
Father of pity, God of grace,
Grant me a vision of Thy face.

With my poor soul now gently share,
Silent intruder, love and care;
Kindly and firmly draw me nigh,
Removing all that caused my sigh.

The grief I caused forgive me, Lord;
Kindly forbear and peace afford;
Pardon and mercy are my plea;
These are the gifts that come from thee.

Slowly my gaze will seek Thine own
And see Thy smile disperse Thy frown:
Full restoration and return,
Repentance Thou wilt never spurn.

Thy healing balm removes the pain
That disobedience must attain;
And I shall love Thy blessèd name,
For Thou hast touched and moved my shame.

# 146

*For consider Him that endured such contradiction of sinners against Himself,*
*lest ye be wearied and faint in your minds.*

Hebrews 12:3

(87.87.D.  Gwynfa)

Saviour, see my spirit failing,
   When my troubled heart is low,
And my fainting understanding
   As the waves of life o'erflow.
Lift mine eyes, O my Redeemer,
   Tell me of Thy great control;
Take my trust from self-endeavour,
   O, to lean on Thee alone!

Give me, Lord, that grace to cherish
   Such a gift that comes from Thee;
Grant a faith that will not perish,
   As displayed at Calvary.
With enlightened understanding,
   Clarity of heart and mind,
Thou dost lead, with love attending
   Every path that I shall find.

In my ways, O Master, guide me,
   Grant a yielding to Thee now;
Bring to mind Thy many mercies,
   As before Thy feet I bow.
Thou art He who changes never,
   For Thou art the Lord supreme;
In a hold that none can sever,
   On Thy sovereign grace I lean.

# 147

*Turn us, O God of our salvation, and cause Thine anger toward us to cease.*

Psalm 85:4

(S.M.  Sarah)

We waited for the Lord,
    And longed His face to see:
We heard the thunder of His Word;
    The love of Calvary

How long, O Lord, shall men
    Defame Thy name in shame?
How long wilt Thou withhold again
    The power of Thy fame?

O come, O Lord, and touch
    With living flame each heart;
Lift up Thy Son, and let Thy church,
    No, never more depart.

Thy presence fills the land
    With fragrance and with fire:
Display Thy strength, stretch forth Thy hand,
    So lift us from the mire.

Now fill our hearts with love,
    A melody of grace:
Celestial notes from heaven above,
    Our songs with joy embrace.

O move the mountains high
    And cause the proud to kneel;
O let our souls to God draw nigh,
    That we Thy presence feel.

## The Christian Life

The time has come at last
  For men to seek the Lord;
Declare Thy truth, to Thee hold fast,
  With Thee with one accord.

Revive Thy work and bring
  The nations to confess
That Thou art Lord, our King of kings,
  Who dost Thy people bless.

# 148

*And the bow shall be in the cloud; and I will look upon it,*
*that I may remember the everlasting covenant between God*
*and every living creature of all flesh that is upon the earth.*

Genesis 9:16

(77.77.  Buckland)

A CHILD'S PRAYER

I, while going on my way,
  Saw a rainbow in the sky;
I remembered God had given
  Words that promised life and heaven.

Rainbow, sign for ever new,
  Red and yellow, green and blue,
In its beauty bright I trace
  Marks of God's unfailing grace.

In my joy I sought to run,
  Nearer to the rainbow come,
But the rainbow would not stay,
  To far regions slipped away.

Now no longer do I raise
In my land glad songs of praise;
Jesus, like the rainbow bright,
Has departed from my sight.

Rainbow, rainbow, O return,
Do not leave me here to mourn;
Jesus, tell me I am Thine,
In my heart forever shine.

*trans. Edmund Owen*

# 149

*Saw ye him who my soul loveth?*
Song of Solomon 3:3
(87.87.D. Moriah)

What is this, the cloud that darkens,
Cloud which hides the Lord above?
What this covering shade that thickens,
Keeps me from the One I love?
Speak, my Jesus, tell what ails me,
May I view again Thy face;
Smile upon me, do not leave me
In distress, O Lord of grace.

Is it mist from off Thy mountain
Makes my heart so cold and drear?
Is it that my Lord is teaching
By declining to draw near?
Speak, my Jesus, what the lesson?
What the message I should heed?
Grant Thine aid and heaven open;
Shed Thy light upon my need.

Is it from the nether regions
  That thick vapours fill the air?
Work of Satan and his legions
  Who would drive me to despair?
Speak, my Jesus, of Thy power,
  Of Thy saving, mighty arm.
To the depths Thy mercy lower
  And deliver me from harm.

*trans. Edmund Owen*

# 150

Based on Isaiah 53.

(C.M. Saron)

All we like sheep have gone astray,
  Each one his own way chose;
So far from God we turned away,
  To Him we seemed like foes.

Yet He in mercy came to save
  The lost and wandering sheep;
The heart of love our sin forgave,
  His precious ones to keep.

On Him iniquity was laid,
  Upon His sinless frame;
The debt for sin was fully paid,
  Our guilt, our sin, our shame.

The Son of God, our shepherd dear,
  Before the shearers stood;
In silence holy, without fear,
  Was slaughtered for our good.

## The Christian Life

The wounds of Christ, eternal worth,
    Moved heaven in wonder— still!
His brutal bruises here on earth
    Fulfilled His Father's will.

Transgressors now in silent awe
    With tears embrace the Son;
The One who satisfied the law
    Salvation now has won.

Despised was He by sinful man,
    Rejected by His kind.
But now believe with loud 'Amen,'
    His grace to those who find.

# 151

Based on Psalm 126.

(66.66.88   Maelor)

When Thou, Lord, didst restore
    Thy people who were kept
In bonds in Babylon—
    For Zion there they wept—
Our dream we scarcely could believe,
That Thou our burden wouldst relieve.

Our mouth Thou then didst fill
    With joy that overflowed;
A new song then we sang
    Of grace Thou hast bestowed.
The nations see, and fear, and own,
The Lord great things for them hath done.

### The Christian Life

The Lord great things hath done
    For us, His ransomed flock;
He brought us from the pit;
    Our feet set on a rock.
Our sins in His own body bore:
For this we'll praise Him evermore.

Our present bondage turn,
    Our state of sore decline;
Meet with Thy people, Lord,
    Revive Thy work again,
That dried-up river beds may now
With living water overflow.

With weeping for lost souls
    Is sown the precious seed;
The sower will return
    With joyful fruit indeed.
The harvest will be gathered in,
Immortal souls, Christ-washed from sin.

# 152

*Christ in you, the hope of glory.*

Colossians 1:27

(76.76.D. Penlan)

Whatever may befall me,
    In this dark world of sin,
I know His blood is o'er me
    Dispelling guilt within.
And when I see His glory,
    I'll give Him all the praise,
And speak of all His mercy,
    Immortal Son of Grace.

# The Christian Life

I have not seen His beauty,
  Nor heard His wondrous voice,
The deep, deep love of Calvary,
  The things of His own choice.
Yet some great day in glory
  I'll fall before His feet,
And then His children glorious
  He graciously will greet.

There is a mind most sovereign
  That knoweth how I feel;
There is a Son most caring
  Who all my wounds will heal.
There is a heart so glorious,
  There is a love so free,
There is a pardon precious
  That seals my all in Thee.

There was a cross most painful,
  There was Gethsemane,
There was a sad betrayal,
  A Saviour's agony.
There is a love that bought me,
  There is a plea for God:
O make me to adore Thee
  And cry for Thee, my Lord.

There is a resurrection
  That God eternal planned,
And now in glory seated,
  The Lord on Thy right hand.
There for me interceding,
  There pleading for my soul,
On Thy right hand now seeing
  The One who made me whole.

# WEDDING HYMNS

# 153

*Except the Lord build the house, they labour in vain that build it.*

Psalm 127:1

(C.M.  Metzler's Redhead)

We worship Thee, the King of grace,
   With heart and soul and voice;
O grant that mercy's smiling face
   May cause us to rejoice!

Along life's path we have been led
   By Thee, our Lord and Friend;
And we have tasted of the Bread
   Of Life, which Thou dost send.

We come to Thee for blessing now
   Upon this wedding-day;
We ask Thee, Lord, Thy grace bestow
   And may Thy presence stay.

We come our promises to make,
   Present our vows to Thee;
Our humble prayer, O gently take,
   That we may faithful be.

Upon our hearts, O grant Thy peace,
   Thy guidance in our lives;
That we may walk the way of grace,
   And be in all things wise.

Upon our home Thy blessing give,
    A haven from the storm,
A place of comfort, where we live
    In harmony and calm.

We look to Thee, our sovereign God,
    For unction and for grace;
And when our journey we have trod,
    We'll see Thy blessèd face.

# 154

*That He might present it to Himself a glorious church, not having spot or wrinkle, or any such thing; but it should be holy and without blemish*
Ephesians 5:27

(C.M.  St. Stephen)

Glory to Thee, O God above,
    For Thou hast loved Thine own.
Thy blessèd Son with costly love,
    Has made us Thine alone.

Thy glorious church while here on earth,
    Is purchased as His bride,
Robed in a righteousness of worth
    Is heaven's delight and pride.

Sweet is the covenant of grace
    Uniting two in Thee;
Love and obedience now embrace
    In happy harmony.

What God has joined for His name's sake
    No man shall separate;
Sacred the promises we make
    Ourselves to consecrate.

## Wedding Hymns

One with each other and with Thee
   In holy unity,
Our lives upon Thine altar be
   In love's captivity.

O grant the presence of the Lord
   To seal the promise rare,
And give the blessing of Thy Word
   With everlasting care.


# 155

*An inheritance incorruptible, and undefiled,*
*and that fadeth not away, reserved in heaven for you.*

1 Peter 1:4

(87.87.D.  Arwelfa)

God eternal in salvation
   Planned a way for man to call;
Found him deep in degradation,
   Ruined twice by sin and Fall.
By election of the Father;
   Sprinkled by our Saviour's blood;
Holy Spirit, Sanctifier —
   See God's plan and mercy's flood!

Precious is the faith God gave us,
   Lasting all the strife of time;
Testing in the fiery furnace,
   All to purge the dross and grime.
Tender see the Master's dealing,
   Purging, cleansing, work Divine;
Spirit teaching, gold refining,
   Till the Saviour's image shine.

Heaven's a home without corruption,
　Undefiled and spotless, pure,
Planned in mercy, God's foundation,
　Word of life, steadfast and sure.
Loving Him with eyes that see not,
　Sight of faith alone can see,
God is our eternal comfort,
　Holy, blessèd Trinity.

# 156

*Heirs together of the grace of life.*
1 Peter 3:7

(87.87.47  Mannheim)

Grant, O Lord, our pure petition
　On this union here to stay;
Give Thy gracious benediction
　On this covenant today.
　　Days of gladness,
　　Days of gladness,
　In their pilgrimage with Thee.

Dear Lord Jesus, guest of honour,
　Take Thy place, adorn with grace,
With Thy presence and Thy favour
　This occasion — now embrace.
　　Precious moments,
　　Precious moments,
　When the feast is filled with Thee.

## Wedding Hymns

O how wondrous is Thy guidance,
   Through the winding ways of life;
Looking at Thy constant count'nance,
   Every step in joy or strife.
      O such friendship,
      O such friendship,
   Resting in Thy tender care.

Blessèd Jesus in Thy mercy
   Seal these promises with power;
Sweetest union, now with beauty,
   Sanctify this solemn hour.
      Glorious cov'nant,
      Glorious cov'nant,
   God ordained for all mankind.

# THE HOLY SCRIPTURES

# 157

*Wherefore I put thee in remembrance that thou stir up the gift of God,*
*which is in thee by putting on of my hands.*

2 Timothy 1:6

(64.64.66.64.  Builth)

Persuaded by Thy word,
    I worship Thee,
Constrained to seek my Lord
    At Calvary.
A burden gone away,
And blessedness to stay,
Removing all dismay:
    I will not flee.

No shame shall wound my heart,
    For Thine embrace
Of peace and power impart
    Sufficient grace.
My life I now commit,
My will to Thee submit,
And at Thy feet I'll sit,
    To seek Thy face.

O grant me strength to hold
    The gospel sweet;
A spirit true and bold
    I gladly greet.
Committed to my care,
A truth beyond compare,
O give me grace to bear:
    Thy foes defeat.

## The Holy Scriptures

When error comes to lie,
  O keep me, Lord;
Then stir Thy gift in me,
  And power afford.
Declare Thy gospel sound,
Destroy when lies abound;
O Jesus, I have found
  Thy word a sword.

# 158

*They that wait upon the Lord shall renew their strength;*
*they shall mount up with wings as eagles;*
*they shall run and not be weary; and they shall walk and not faint.*

Isaiah 40:31

(77.77.D.  Aberystwyth)

Everlasting is the Word
  Strong in power and rich in grace;
Every promise of the Lord
  Shines with glory from His face.
Never weary in His way
  Is the King who made the earth;
Great Creator, who dost sway
  Sovereign rule and priceless worth.

To the faint He giveth aid;
  To the weak a way of joy;
Strong shall faint and young shall fade,
  Yet His grace shall love employ.
Blessèd is our happy place,
  He has moved the darkness dim;
See His mercy as we trace
  Love and justice dwell in Him.

## The Holy Scriptures

They that on the Lord do wait,
    Now mount up with eagle's flight—
Wings of majesty so great,
    Glorious is the wondrous sight.
They shall run and never tire;
    They shall walk and never fall;
For the Lord is their desire,
    God of grace and all in all.

# 159

*In whom we have redemption through His blood the forgiveness of sins.*

Ephesians 1:7

(73.73.77.73.73.  Cymod)

There is a path of pardon
    In His blood;
There is a sure salvation
    In His blood.
A law's full consummation,
A Father's approbation —
Hear Zion's acclamation!
    In His blood —
Atonement and redemption
    In His blood!

O come, ye sons of Adam,
    And rejoice!
Now trust the God of Abraham
    And rejoice!
O hasten, happy sinner,
To life in Christ for ever,
To bonds that nought can sever:
    O rejoice!
In full and glad surrender
    O rejoice!

William Williams (Llanbrynmair)

# 160

*Neither is there salvation in any other: for there is none other name under heaven given among men, whereby we must be saved.*

Acts 4:12

(C.M.  Saron)

There's none but Jesus, beauteous Lord,
    Can fill this heart of mine
With comforts sweet and kind accord,
    From depths of death divine.

No other one, with such delight,
    Can fill my troubled breast;
I often gaze upon that sight,
    And in His merits rest.

In His rich wounds I see a place
    My guilty head to hide,
For there I'll find sufficient grace,
    And in His arms abide.

The price He paid, my soul has found,
    And rests secure in love;
For there upon redemption ground,
    I'll claim my home above.

William Rees v.1,2 & 3
William Jones v.4

# 161

*Whom having not seen, ye love.*

1 Peter 1:8

(87.87.D.  Corinth)

Lord of grace and power, I love Thee,
 Yet unseen to human sight:
Thou didst draw my soul with mercy
 From its dearest false delight.
In a moment Thou didst conquer
 What the world could not achieve;
Now enthroned in silent splendour
 In my heart as I believe.

Heart and mind and sight and hearing,
 Never thought or ever knew
Of the wonder of Thy Being,
 Absolute, profound and true.
Yet I find my heart doth love Thee,
 More than all in nature's world;
Greater news and sweeter mercy,
 Is Thy Person to behold.

Highest heaven is Thy abiding,
 Far above the span of mind.
Sinful depths of sorrow hiding
 In the home of man I find.
Yet I know my soul is nearer
 To my Lord, and stranger still
Is Thy promise, and far dearer
 Than the world with all its skill.

William Williams (Pantycelyn)

# 162

*These all died in faith, not having received the promises, but having
seen them afar off, and were persuaded of them, and embraced them,
and confessed that they were strangers and pilgrims on the earth.*

Hebrews 11:13

(87.87.D. Arwelfa)

Let my rest in thee be peaceful
　'Neath the palm trees of Thy love;
Let me rest with pilgrims faithful
　On their path to heaven above.
There relate Thy faithful mercies
　In the wilderness we face,
Then forget our great distresses
　As we praise Thy powerful grace.

O how sweet a company travelling
　With their gaze fixed on their home;
Not a tongue in malice piercing,
　Not a heart with guile may roam.
See the dew on souls descending,
　Hear their confidence in Him,
Listen to their heartfelt longing
　As they love to speak of heaven.

Hold me, Lord, in all my travelling,
　There is little left at best;
On my soul Thy sunshine warming,
　Bidding me at last to rest.
Let the breeze of heaven so gently
　Touch me, keep me, from all ill,
Yet my feet now standing firmly
　On the heights of Zion's hill.

*Ambrose Williams*
*trans. William Vernon Higham*

# INDEX TO HYMNS

First line of each verse is listed with bold type indicating first line of hymn

# Index

# Index

# Index

# Index

# Index

# Index

# Index

# Index

# Index

# Index

# Index

# Index

# Index

# Index

# Index

# Index

# Index

# Index

## Index

# Tentmaker Publications

\* \* \* \* \* \* \*

TENTMAKER PUBLICATIONS was set up in 1993 with the aim of supporting Irish believers working in the Republic of Ireland as pastors and evangelists. Many evangelical churches in the Republic are small and unable to fully support their own pastors. With this in mind we have followed the pattern of the Apostle Paul and hence the name Tentmaker, from Paul's practice of supporting himself on the mission field by making tents.

Our books are reproduced using modern technology and are printed in small runs thus allowing us to publish works which otherwise might not be reprinted. The costs of production are higher as a proportion of selling price and we rely substantially on direct sales to the customer. Whilst many of our publications are distributed through shops, some are only available direct from the publishers.

If you would like to support this venture and receive a free newsletter giving details of new publications and discount offers, please write to us at:

**Tentmaker Publications**
**121 Hartshill Road,**
**Stoke-on-Trent,**
**Staffs.**
**ST4 7LU**
**U.K.**

**E-mail: Tentmaker@Compuserve.com**